·❋*❋*·*·*❋*❋*·*

That We
Be
one

*✳✳✳✳**✳✳✳*

That We
Be
one

ron bianco

.****.***.

That We

Be

one

Printed United States of America
ISBN-10: 0692203656
ISBN-13: 978-0692203651

Cover Design by Ron

REVISED EDITION (Feb. 2016)

Text: Baskerville O F ... Headings: Brush Script MT ... Title: Wide Latin

ADDITIONAL COPIES AVAILABLE
BY CONTACTING THE EMAIL ADDRESS BELOW

thatwebeone@gmail.com
thatwebeone.com

Dedication

It is to Sandra Lee Scolari
a sister in Christ whom I love dearly
that I dedicate this book and it's message.

For it is she
who I've come to believe
God used as His instrument
to question, and to goad me
on matters of faith and Scripture.

Provoking me as she did,
I came to search and scrutinize the Scriptures
all the more seriously than I had ever done.

Thus have I prayed and my faith roused
as I found in them the fullness of faith
and of trust.

Thank you God

Thank you Sandy

* Acknowledgements *

My thanks to teacher Julie Parker whose most studious corrections of my grammar were so needed (gotta admit, I didn't heed 'em all); to Dr. Greg Pierce, Dr. of Theology, Southern Baptist Ministry and Biblical Studies, for his encouragement (along with his quote of Psalms119:165, "*Great peace have they which love thy law: and nothing shall offend them*"); to Pastor Jim Truax for his caring spirit; to Forest St. Pierre, a Eucharistic Minister and Confirmation Instructor at Sts. John & Paul Parish of Coventry, RI, for his humbling and most appreciated testimony; to Father John Kita for his blessing and attention to doctrine (though I have since added text); to Devin Rose for his advice (author of: 'The Protestant Dilemma'); to Mr. Webber and Mr. Rice for their album, 'Jesus Christ Superstar' that, in spite of its heretical aspects (that many condemned), the passion portrayed by the Christ character (and so too Judas), got me to wondering secretly within, could this divinity and resurrection of Christ be true? To Ernest 'Gip' Cabral who was first to really penetrate my heart to the Gospel: Gip's sincerity, and respect, as he spoke of God's love diffused my resistance (Ha! no "free business lunch" to be had from this salesman); and to all the priests who gave of their care and attention throughout the years ... most especially Archbishop George Pierce, who so silently listened to me for hours and hours, and read long letters to him of circumstances in my life ... as well as my many blunt statements, questions and concerns about God, Christ, truth, and faith. An amazing priest.

That We
Be
one

* Contents *

That We
Be
one

*✳✱✳✱.✱✳✳✱

Preface

In my own search, and indeed I really gotta say, my immensely impassioned quest for the truth of life's meaning and purpose, I considered so so many a way!

I'm in my senior years now as I write you here (went by so fast). My youthful "immortality" has departed me. For a good part of my adult years, especially it's onset, I was more or less atheistic/agnostic, and very anti-Christian. This conviction allowed me in my life to pretty much ignore my conscience, and carryon in whatever behavior I chose ... some of it very sinful. There were sins that I embraced as acceptable, even righteous, and those I was simply unwilling to give up.

It's not that all my ways were prone to sin. There is much in me that I recognize as compassionate, being of a good heart, and helping those in need in some way or other. A particular trait of mine, and that I privately pondered as somehow being of meaningful import in the very core of my character, was a propensity to cry (to my embarrassment, and that of others as well) whenever I'd see good win out over the bad in a movie, for instance; or where I'd see love prevail; or someone sacrificing themselves in some manner or other, for another; or any act that brings to light the intrinsic goodness in mankind that I believe is within us ... most especially is this so in watching any movie about Christ and viewing His goodness, His forgiveness, His miracles, and His words. Viewing His crucifixion has me bawling uncontrollably. And even real good music, singing, and harmonies could bring me to tears (such as done by Jackie Evancho). This disposition continues to this day.[1]

I am repentant nowadays of any sins, and thankful of my being completely dependent on God's mercy. Mercy I don't deserve; though I do hope for, ask for, and gratefully accept.[2] Thank you God.

Truly, I have come to be aware of, and acknowledging here, just how good God has been to me throughout my life, even when in unrepentant sin ... for there I was, typical of the world, engulfed in an everyday persuasion of lusts, pride, greed, hidden fears, contempt, and unfaithfulness. I was legion.[3]

I recognize now His faith in me as well as His tolerance; all the things He has rescued me from, all the harm and punishments I could otherwise have faced. When I first came to recognize the love of God revealed in Christ, I cried. What an understatement!!! That I should be the recipient of this divine love, to grasp the genuineness of this mercy so way beyond my understanding, brought me

---

[1] As an example, the movie, 'The Notebook' had me bawling. So too, did I cry watching 'ET', along with many, many, many others. Even the song, 'America the Beautiful' brings me to tears.

[2] Psalms51:3-6, 12-14, 17

[3] To paraphrase C.S. Lewis from his book, 'Surprised By Joy'.

to bawling a sob of sobs pouring out from my very soul it seems, that I could not at all hold back. It was repentance-and-gratitude. I'll never forget this cry. It was cathartic beyond measure.

It is said in the Scriptures that to whom much has been given, much is required.[4] *This is exactly how I feel* ... that God has done all this for me; and done so for a reason. I am grateful, and feel I ought to *do* something to really give thanks. Just what that may be, I'm unsure, but in part, it is certainly why I am motivated to write this book and share it with you.

In all honesty, having lived as I have, though not absent of goodness and love of course, I still have a lot of nerve to think I can now make comment on the Christian faith. I can't claim I'm a model Christian. Nor am I a theologian of any sort. Some could say, and perhaps rightly so, that I'm writing of such things which I know far too little about. I nevertheless feel obliged of heart to express my thoughts and reasoning in this book. I wake up each and every morning, eager to write, and many days spending hours upon hours doing so. Such is my concern:

It began in my thirties that I came to noticing that there was possibly more going on in life than met the eye. Boy, was this so very, very divergent to my way of looking at things. Having an engineering education, I was prone to scrutinizing things in a rather scientific-mathematical-and

---

[4] Luke12:48

probability manner. As I mentioned, I came in time to really wanting to know the truth. Was there a purpose? Just what was life all about? I recall one night, while lying comfortably in bed, and thinking about life, and death, and as if not even of my own doing, I spoke out so softly in a child-like whimpering voice: "I don't want to die." I didn't just mean my earthly death, I meant I couldn't fathom my coming to an oblivion[5] (I knew this came from deep within).

I looked upon and read many psychologies, philosophies and religions throughout these years. These ranged from an embracing of the hippie culture (seeking therein may be a utopia), to Hare Krishna, the Moonies, Scientology, to Christianity, and certainly the various pagan ways of life. From the west coasts to east coasts, I attended various meetings, seminars, tent revivals, philosophical presentations, and read many books offering various viewpoints and beliefs. Some had something to offer, but I felt were incomplete, especially about life's meaning and purpose, lacking as well any substantial explaining of death and beyond (if there was).

I'll tell you about one in particular, which I recall so well, for it was so silly (and I mention it here to you only that you too may get the same chuckle of it that I did at the time): The belief of this group was that the pyramid shape had the means within it to focus the power of the universe under its dome which would bring peace and enlightenment to those within it (discovered by the

---

[5] I did not appreciate then that my existence is eternal, be it in heaven or hell.

Pharaohs of long ago they pointed out – which is why they built the great pyramids as their place of burial). So ... its adherents ... *well* ... would you believe, they wore wire framed pyramids, the size of a hat, upon their heads? Seeing them do so, I could not refrain myself in grinning from ear to ear even as I tried so not to humiliate them. In that I knew not of their belief and ways prior, I only attended that one presentation (and besides, I don't like hats).

In a more serious tone, what all this amounted to was a dire quest, I mean a deep, deep, deep hunger, an insistence, to know, if knowing was possible, the truth ... no matter, no matter, no matter, where it led me. A period of gloom engulfed me for a time as I began to grasp that there was something wrong in our world, with people, with me (though in hindsight, it motivated me to dig further into life's meaning and purpose). It was in that state of mind and heart where I began to truly ask in a most serious and sincere way: what's it all about? I view that period now as substantially good, as I was now humbled as I went through effort after effort which continued on now for several more years in my search for life's meaning. On occasion I wrote some songs that were acutely introspective and so solemnly questioning of life, my existence, my thoughts and wants, my hopes and dreams, and God's existence ... in which I poured out my heart, and my many tears.

There then came a convergence of frustrations! *"What the heck was the truth?"* All this searching and questioning; all this wondering; all my ponderings and musings; all these meetings and presentations; the tent revivals; in conjunction with Scripture and all the numerous and varied books read; my personal ponderings and introspections; contemplations; deliberations; conversations; even the arguments; which of them was I to believe ... if any of em? It had reached for me a point of a distressing heartfelt exasperation! I was riled up within so much, that one evening at home, as I happened to be sitting on the floor, and feeling so discouraged and annoyed in thinking about all this, I began lightly pounding my fists on the floor, speaking out as I did (getting progressively louder and my pounding all the harder): *"I wanna know the truth !"* ... *"I wanna know the truth !!!"* ... ... *"I wanna know the truth !!!!!"*

There were a range of circumstances, some from introspection and reflection, some a bit traumatic, some a bit extraordinary, and some from just plain thinking and discussing of such matters, that led me to come to a hope, and call upon God, and upon Christ. Indeed it was, that I got to my knees and spoke out to a God that I was not at all sure existed. I felt at the time, that raw honesty was going to be the manner in which I ought to speak, such that my initial words were: "I think this is foolish..." then I made a request for the truth, if there were such a thing.

As time went on, I did come to be inclined to pray (rather infrequently). I came as well to looking upon the Scriptures and the many Christian denominations. Of course I saw their commonality, but I noticed too, disparities in their beliefs; in their doctrines, in their moralities, and in their very faiths. Some of these differences were slight and some were not slight at all.

But this book is not about me, and it is as well time for me to now leave the past behind ... looking forward to the hope which God has offered me: My sincere hope here is to portray from my heart, the distinctions and divisions I see in Christianity ... and my concern.

With deep sincerity and humility do I ask: That you please read this book (most especially the chapter on 'No Doubt') ... *even as some of it may be bothersome to you by my unbridled way at times.*[6]

If what I write here can do just this one thing, I am grateful to God to have written it: That you pray for the unity of the Christian faith. We need to be one.

---

[6] Note that some of what I write is in broad generalities, and will surely not be relating to each denomination and every reader.

That We
Be
one

∗✳✳∗∗✳✳∗∗

The Matter of Comparison

In comparing the Christian faiths, it was apparent that the Scriptures can be, and are, used to support con interpretations. In our efforts for spiritual truths, we come across this as we witness that there are many Christian denominations throughout the world.

As there exist now in my life close relations with a family of the Baptist faith, (whom I love and who treat me so kindly), my comparisons here will tend more with this denomination as I've come to note and understand it's beliefs a bit more so than others.

To begin with, I see how Baptist teach that only Christ can forgive sin (for there is only one mediator between God and man, 1Tim2:5, they point out). Yet, I read that right after Christ breaths upon the apostles giving them, thus, the Holy Spirit, He says to them in Jn.20:23: *"Whose soever sins ye remit, they are remitted unto them; and whose soever sins ye retain, they are retained."* [7]

---

[7] John20:23; Mt.16:19, 18:18

What is Jesus meaning to say here? Might we speculate, in a lighthearted, though serious of a manner, what the apostles themselves thought about what Jesus had said to them:

> "Did Jesus just say, we can forgive people of their sins; or not do so, as we may choose?" questioned Mark of the others. "Can't be!" says James with a bit of insistence, "Jesus merely said, *'whose sins we remit, they are remitted; and whose we retain they are retained'.*" "I don't see how we can take that to mean that we can forgive sins, even in His name." "What then do you think He meant?" Mark asked him in utter bewilderment. "Well", says John, "He only meant that, whose sins we remit, they are remitted; and whose we don't, they are not." "Now wait, wait, wait! Can't you see He only says we can 'remit' 'em!" adds Matthew in the discussion. "To remit", he points out, "means to pay someone; you know, as in 'remittance". "You guys are really getting carried away to think the Lord would give to us the power to forgive sins. No matter that He has all authority in heaven and on earth!" "We can remit em, that's all!" continued Mark. "Do not, I tell you, think otherwise!" asserted Matthew most unyieldingly. Now this, well it absolutely infuriated Phillip! "Why do you not believe what Jesus just told us?" He shouted at

Matthew! "We can forgive sin! That's what He said!!! Why do you seek to second guess our Lord???" shouted Phillip, all the more!!! Then in a calmer tone, Phillip continues: "Look, whatever Jesus says, if you believe in Him, then just trust Him. What right or knowledge have we to be doubting what Jesus told us so directly?" he asked. "C'mon guys, is He not wiser than us? Is He not the Son of God?" A solemn and reflective reserve overcame them; as Peter, though unspoken throughout, listened intently, as he prayed in seeking God's will.

Baptists, and Protestants in general, are taught these words of Christ mean not what they appear to say. I just don't know how someone can come up with any way to reason out that these words of our Lord do not mean He is telling those He is speaking to that they can forgive sins? Nonetheless, many do. If you ask me, it seems they feel obliged to find some way, just someway, to make it not mean what He is saying. Why are they so bent out of shape over this? It's Jesus Christ, the Lord of the whole universe, saying it; why not just believe Him? Why can't they submit themselves to this commandment? It's right there, as clear as day, in the Bible. But they just don't. Instead they'll search for something, for anything; there's just got to be some Scripture somewhere that they can point to and insist it is supportive of their disbelief (but note that the New Testament Scripture does not yet even exist at that time).

"Only Christ can forgive sins!" Baptist and others so adamantly pronounce. Christ, Himself, they point out, says that He has the power to forgive sins.[8] "God doesn't need a priest in order to forgive me!" they vehemently say. No He doesn't. Nevertheless, as is quite clearly stated in God's word, Christ established this down-to-earth means; for He knew (I've no doubt) how profoundly it would work. He knew what an outpouring and trustful opening of the human heart could occur given this means of confessing one's sin to one so ordained to have this heavenly gift of absolving someone of their sins in His authority (for no one has the ability to bridge the gap of sin between God and man but Jesus Christ).

As Paul writes in 2Cor.5:18: *"All things are of God, who hath reconciled us to himself by Jesus Christ, and hath given to us the ministry of reconciliation."* (take note, that this ministry-of-reconciliation of which Paul writes, is not only for him, but for those elders in the church to whom he has addressed his letter). Why ignore this, or try to spin this ministry of reconciliation which Paul writes of here in some challenging and opposing way ... such as thinking that what Paul means here is that all Christians have this ministry in reconciling people to Christ by their evangelizing (as a Baptist pastor so preached one afternoon)? This is quite a stretch! Paul was speaking to Timothy here; not to you, not to me, not to every Christian in the world. So too, Scriptures state that Jesus was speaking to particular disciples of His when He gave

---

[8] Mk.2:10; Mt.9:6; 1Jn.2:2; Lk.23:24; Ps.86:5

to these ministers of His church, and only these ministers of His church, the literal and faithful *ministry of reconciliation;* thus it is for them, and only them, to actually have, by His authority, the Godly ordained capacity to forgive a repentant of their sins. Why the seeking to refute this when it is so clearly spoken of by Christ in the Bible?

I personally do ponder, if for some who refuse to believe that Christ meant what He said here, might it be that they feel a personal insult about confessing their sins to another person (who is a sinner as well)? In their refusal, are they simply finding it too difficult to accept these words of Christ and faithfully submit themselves in this way? "How arrogant!" they adamantly protest, "that it is for another human being to think he can absolve me of sin!" Might theirs be a heart unwilling to surrender in faith to the teachings of Christ ... or too timid ... or too proud?

Imagine with me now, if you will, that we travel back to that time, and you observe me as I walk up to Jesus just after He's said this to these men, and I say very reverently to Him: "Lord, I know that what you just said to them doesn't mean that they can forgive anyone of their sins." Though He's quoted: " *Whose sins ye remit they are remitted...",* how do I substantiate my knowledge of what He intends? Honestly, what do I say to Him of why *I know* He did not mean they can forgive sins? What, might we conjecture would be His reply to me? What do you think He should reply to me?

In my comparisons, I saw too that many Christian

denominations teach that Christ is speaking symbolically as He proclaims the bread that He raised in blessing is His body, and the drink is His Blood, to be eaten and drank; done in remembrance of Him. [9] A Baptist pastor tells me that, were it not symbolic, it would have meant for those present to then eat Him. [10] Good grief! Jesus does not say to eat His arm or leg. He says to eat of the bread and drink, and that the bread and drink are His body and His blood. He even refers to the bread as *"His flesh"*, and that without our eating of it, He asserts we have no life. What a dire a thing to say to them (and to us)! And while Jesus is quoted as referring to His declarations here as being, *"a new testament"*,[11] most Protestants, refer to them, as being "symbolic" (quite a disparity). Aren't they here denying the power of God to do this by their lack of recognition? [12]

Those who were literal disciples as Jesus spoke of this became so troubled by what He was stating, that even though they witnessed many of His miraculous deeds, His changing water into wine! His walking on water! Healing the sick! Bringing sanity back to the insane! Raising some from the dead! Having mastery over the

---

[9] Jn.6:48-68

[10] To be honest, my initial reaction to his saying this, was bleak and frustrating, for how silly and lacking in serious dialogue I felt he evidently was in debating the truth here in a sincere manner. I've since sought to give him some slack ... and more regard.

[11] Mt.26:26-28; Mk.14:22-24; Lk.22:18-20; ; Heb.9:15(note here that "testament" can be equated with "covenant").

[12] 2Tim.3:5

forces of nature in calming the waters (to name but a few), they still left Him because of what He was saying. Isn't this incredible? Is it not bizarre that they left Jesus, as a consequence of this "symbolism"?

Isn't it hard to believe they would leave Him, whom they believed to be the Lord, merely because of a symbolic reference by Him?

Evidently they who left, and very much to their consternation, did take Him literally and seriously; believing He meant what He was saying; and meant it literally. To boot, we read as well that Christ makes no effort at all to explain further to them, that He might bring them back. Rather He asserts Himself all the more in this matter! Nor does His comment in Jn.6:43, *"It is the spirit that quickeneth; the flesh profiteth nothing: the words that I speak unto you, they are spirit, and they are life"* in any way clarify it for them have or have any persuasion upon them to believe He did not mean what He was saying to be taken literally. Christ goes beyond even His asserting Himself all the more to those who are leaving Him, but He makes an extraordinary comparison to them of His statements with the miracle of His ascension (Jn.6:62). Would such a daring comparison as this be made of mere symbolism? It hardly seems so. Indeed, Christ does speak in metaphors and symbolism at times, but there is no departing of anyone from Him at those times; and oftentimes He goes on to describe and further explain such things as being metaphors.

To look upon this discourse of His, and the reactions of

those present, along with His response to them, and as well His lack of response, how can we now, some two-thousand years later, ever think we understand what Jesus meant better than they who were right there ... they who heard, not only His words, but His tone of voice and witnessed His demeanor, experiencing all this as they did first-hand?

I don't want my being blunt to be offensive, but I've got to say, someone has to have a lot of moxie to go up to Christ and say to Him that the bread and the drink He just blessed, are not His body and His blood, when He just said they are. He says: "*This is my body.*" Who would say? "No it isn't." Many do.

As Scripture points out here, it was found to be *a hard saying* by many who were there at the time (many today are in agreement with them). But for us at this time, with all four of the Gospel writers mentioning these very words of Christ,[13] and not a one of them saying anything about their being symbolic, not even a hint, what-oh-what is the impasse in believing Jesus here? Even Paul, in his mentioning of the body and blood in his letter to those in the Corinthian church, as well gives no indication whatsoever of his reference being symbolic. He does quite the opposite (don't you think?), for he gives them a most serious and stern warning in his letter to them, and I quote him in full, as he wrote: "*For I have received of the Lord that which also I delivered unto you, That the Lord*

---

[13] Luke22:19; Mt.26:26; Mk.14:22; John6:54

Jesus the same night in which He was betrayed took bread: And when he had given thanks, he brake it, and said, Take, eat: this is my body, which is broken for you: this do in remembrance of me. After the same manner also he took the cup, when he had supped, saying, This cup is the new testament in my blood: this do ye, as oft as ye drink it, in remembrance of me. For as often as ye eat this bread, and drink this cup, ye do shew the Lord's death till he come.” (notice the magnitude that Paul is placing upon the words of Christ, as he quotes them so explicitly). He must surely see these words, as particularly significant and vital instructions from Christ). Paul then adds, *“Wherefore whosoever shall eat this bread, and drink this cup of the Lord, unworthily, shall be guilty of the body and blood of the Lord.”* even he goes on to say, as in warning; *“For he that eateth and drinketh unworthily, eateth and drinketh damnation to himself, not discerning the Lord's body.”*[14] Those are strong words of warning coming from Paul. Would he speak in this manner about symbolism? Can you picture Paul saying: *“For he that eateth and drinketh this symbolism unworthily, eateth and drinketh damnation to himself, not discerning the symbolism of the Lord's body”?*

Jesus refers to what He is telling the disciples here as *“the new testament”*;[15] to reduce then His new-testament-instructions to being merely symbolic, sure is inconsistent with the very exalted regard that Jesus gives to this co-union with Him in His blessing of the bread and wine as

---

[14] 1Cor.11:23-29 A testament is akin to a covenant.
[15] 1Cor.11:23-29

His body and blood. Indeed, why would He bless the bread and wine if He meant only that they are just symbolic objects to be taken only in a remembrance of Him?

The Catholic Church, on the other hand, does not minimize His words as mere symbolism. Rather, how radically different is there belief as they teach and take His proclamations here with such great acclamation, with no ifs; with no ands; with no buts. They *do* exactly as He instructs, and in faith and trust, this belief in the words of Christ are at the very heart of the Catholic worship service ... the Mass.

Reiterating the same words, even the very gestures[16] of Jesus at His last supper, the priest speaks and carries them out to God and the congregation as he raises the bread ... just as Jesus did ... gives blessing ... just as Jesus did ... gives thanks to God ... just as Jesus did ... breaks the bread ... just as Jesus did ... and just as Jesus did, he speaks out, *"Take this, all of you, and eat of it, for this is my body..."*

Similarly, the priest raises the chalice ... just as Jesus did ... he gives thanks to God ... just as Jesus did ... saying just as Jesus did, *"Take this, all of you, and drink from it, for this is the chalice of my blood ... this do in remembrance of me."*

As Jesus said of the bread: *"This is my body"* ... the priests do indeed believe it is His body. As Jesus said of

---

[16] Inasmuch as His actions are described in the Scriptures.

the drink: *"This is my blood"*... they do indeed believe it is His blood; and as this eternally sacred and ancient ritual is performed by the priests, a ritual which was initiated by Christ at His last Passover supper, this miracle takes place[17] at each and every Catholic Mass throughout the world.

Thus, in my comparison I saw a conviction of simple, yet so profound a faith taught by the Catholic Church ... not only *in Christ*, but a faith, a trust, in His every instruction, His every commandment, His every word, even His every gesture; exalting them as sacred, and never, never seeking to minimizing them.[18]

This so impressed me.

---

[17] Many dismiss this miracle believing it is nothing but hocus-pocus, thus do they reject the power of God as written of in 2Tim.3:5, and in accord with the following Scriptures: Matt.26:26; Mk.14:12; Lk.22:19; 1Cor.10:16-17; 11:24.

[18] I am so flawed and deficient in my aspiration to pass this on to you. I'm sorry I am for it must hinder, in ways even unseen, what my heart seeks to convey. I pray to come from love ... for this I do believe, as Scripture says: Not to love, is not to know God (1John4:8, 4:16; 1Cor.13:1-13).

That We
Be
one

✳✳✳✳✳✳✳✳

The Matter of Reverence

Here is an experience of mine sometimes while at Mass:

Sitting in the pew, as the service was beginning, I silently within began to cry: A few tears rolled down my cheeks. "Why was I crying?" I asked of myself. The answer was clear to me: I was crying because of the reverence for God, for Christ, and for the Bible and its Scripture, that I saw so manifest in this service. Even too, just in how people were behaving; it was as if they had a sense, so personal to each of them, of being in a place that was sacred.[19]

Before the service began, upon entering the church, I saw some parishioners sitting silently in the pews. Some were kneeling. They were in prayer. No one came to greet me, to chat, or ask my name, or give their regards in any a way (beyond perhaps a head nod) ... for when coming together in the Mass, this being a most special act of our Christian worship, there is a yearning to be delivered from all that is casual. It is not even to hear someone preach whom we come for; but we come to the center of all that is: *We come to Christ.* The attitude and

---

[19] 1Tim.3:15

attention is on reverence to God, such that there is a sacredness of sorts to one's indistinctness here. I noticed too, as each parishioner entered, their very first response was to their Creator as a triune God, with the sign of the cross, doing so in the name of the Father, the Son, and the Holy Spirit.

As the service began, the priest in procession with others walked down the aisle towards the altar. The Bible is held high. Behind him was carried the cross with the crucified Christ. Then reaching the altar, the priest gave it a light kiss. "Why would he do such a thing?" It is because here upon this altar will take place the once-and-for-all holy and redeeming sacrifice of Christ. A sacrifice that is perpetual, and on this altar, will it be re-presented ... *for it is eternal.*

The priest then spoke, reminding us that we come before God in the name of the complete trinity of God; the Father; the Son; and the Holy Spirit. We are to call to mind, he says, that we are sinners, and to ask for God's mercy. A sinner's prayer is confessed aloud collectively by all (similar to, though elaborated a bit more, than the Protestant version). There were then readings from the Psalms; the congregation as well spoke some out collectively. A reading followed from the Old Testament; then Scripture was read from one of the epistles (note that these weren't done in a one-two-three cryptic fashion as it may so sound by my mentioning of them one after another like this).

Following these Scriptural readings, the congregation stood for the next reading: *The Gospel.* The priest then recited the day's Gospel (this same is read at all Catholic churches in every nation throughout the world on this day in keeping with Paul's instructions that we be of one accord).[20] When the Gospel's reading was completed, the priest kissed the Bible.

All in all there were four Bible readings. The priest then went to the altar. There he raised the bread, and acknowledged the Scripture and words of Christ spoken at His last supper:[21] "Jesus took bread, said the blessing, and broke it, and gave it to his disciples, and said, *'Take and eat; this is my body.'*" the priest then raised the cup, again speaking the Scriptural account and the Words of Christ, saying, "In a similar manner, He took the cup, and gave thanks, and gave it to them, saying; *'Drink ye all of it; for this is my blood of the new testament, which will be shed for many, for the remission of sins. Do this in remembrance of me.'*" [22] The priest is actually *doing,* I repeat for emphasis, he's *doing* , not only speaking, expressly what Christ did and commanded. In essence, it was the Bible in action.

Everyone is silent; so so silent. And everyone's kneeling. Many have their heads bowed; and the silence seems

---

[20] Phil.2:2 Some speak against this Catholic unity throughout the world as not then allowing the Holy Spirit to spontaneously lead the readings of the pastor. The church, on the other hand, in accordance with the Word of God in 1Cor.1:10 & 11-12, *that ye all speak the same thing,* does just as is commanded throughout all the nations of the world.

[21] Though I quote, there is some inconsequential paraphrasing here.

[22] Mt.26:26-28; Lk.22:19-20; Mk.14:22-24; 1Cor.11:23-29

somehow momentous. Just what is going on?

That truth be told, it is believed by the congregation, and as presented by the priest, that a divine act, you know, the miracle Scripture makes mention of, well it's about to take place: *"Behold the Lamb of God, who takes away the sins of the world"*, says the priest, as he raises high the body and the blood of Christ (in the form of bread and wine). Surely doesn't look like a miracle. It doesn't feel like a miracle; and when I go to the altar, the divine presence of Christ comes to be offered to me and is upon my tongue, it only tastes like bread! So too, the drink tastes like sweet wine! *So where's the miracle???*

It's in the authority of God, and the Eucharistic revelation of Christ. It's in God's words. It's in the acceptance of this as a divine gift from God, and a most humble one indeed it is, because the Lord said it is what it is ... that He may dwell *in* us, and we *in* Him, literally. For those who have such faith, this sacramental meal is offered and celebrated in all the Masses throughout all the world. Again there is here the Bible, not only in word, but in action.

Certainly the bodily presence of the risen Christ in the Eucharist is a mystery that can never be fully explained even by the church. We must bear in mind that God is the Creator of all that exists, and though I know it goes without saying, He has the power to do more than we can ever possibly imagine.

Just as God transcends time, the blood of Jesus shed on the cross transcends time. This sacrifice of Christ is for all time, and its purpose is accomplished once and for all as Christ proclaimed: It is finished. Jesus does not sacrifice Himself again and again upon the altar (as some do accuse). Rather, it is in this time-transcendent way, by the power of the Holy Spirit, that Christ is offered upon the altar.[23] Just as in the Passover meal, the sacrificial lamb is eaten ... so too, as John the Baptist declared: Christ is *"the Lamb of God."* [24]

Now some, most rightly so, point out that Jesus said He would be with us always, and that wherever two or more are gathered in His name, He is present.[25] Are there not though differences in His presence to us? For an example: When the apostles and His mother were in the upper room and Jesus appeared bodily. Prior to His factual entrance, He was there, though unseen, just as He said. But oh boy, when He actually appeared physically before them, and asked to be touched even, you can bet His "presence" surely reached a far more enthralling, captivating, and impactful manifestation to them ... don't you think?

Yes, I did cry silently within as I observed all this reverence to God. What a faith in believing, and in doing, really *doing*, exactly that which Jesus told us to do while having His very last supper on earth. That Christ spoke of this at such a momentous and solemn a time in His ministry, knowing that so soon would He be mocked, tortured, and crucified, points out all the more

---

[23] Ex.12:24, Heb.10:8-10
[24] John1:29
[25] Mt.18:20

that His mentioning this is of a most meaningful consequence.

Yes, I cried for I took to heart what a God we have. How He willingly accepted this sacrifice, and that He would leave us with this communion to having His body and blood, available to us; said by Jesus Christ, Himself, to be *His bread of life.* How fitting this ritual ceremony, so right and so proper, of our Lord's sacred offering; just one of those rituals which are for many, reason to ridicule the Catholic church. But for the Catholic they are rituals of worship and faith. Oh yes! I can see why some laugh at the church's ways. But for us Catholics ... it's no joke.

Some denominations teach that the body and blood is whatever one thinks 'em to be. That it is a personal decision. Hence for some, it is the body and blood; but for others, even of the same denomination and church, it is merely representing His body and blood. How can this possibly be? Come on! Either it's the body and blood of the Lord, or it's not; and if it is, it's a miraculous act of God's will, not one accomplished by the recipient's belief. If it were not, no personal decision could ever make it so. As for the Catholic church, one of her first steps in faith is to a humility and an unhesitating trust to that *which Christ says it is.* No wrangling. No second-guessing. No splitting of hairs. He said it is, so it is.

The Mass is a sacred and mystical act.[26] It is an act of devotion and worship unto God; led, as it is, by the priest and enjoined by all in the congregation that are so willing, without reserve or hesitation, to go beyond their own human understanding in accepting the words and instructions of Jesus Christ. Having a faith, as Paul describes to the church in Corinth, that is not by the words of a psychologically compelling and charismatic speaker, or by the emotional persuasions of a theatrical preacher, but a faith that has the very participation of the Holy Spirit, just as Paul wrote of in 1Cor.2:4. Some, though viewing these rituals of faith, do not recognize this ... believing them instead to be "hocus-pocus".[27]

Yes, there were tears upon my cheeks, for so heartrending it is to see our Father in heaven, whose love is so profound for mankind, so willingly to suffer, even for wretched me, being given such reverence.

At one point in the Mass, we collectively prayed the Lord's Prayer; here too, the comparison I came to noticing is whereby there are denominations teaching that the reply of Jesus when asked how to pray, was but a suggestion or model; the Catholic exalts it and proclaims it to be a commandment ... the one teaching a minimal interpretation; the other elevating it to its highest.

Suppose Christ were at your home, sitting in your living

---

[26] Thus, Mass is capitalized (consider too the birth date of Christ being celebrated as Christ-mas)

[27] Referring to the Eucharist in this way is a grave sin: As Christ said on the cross, "Forgive them Father, for they know not what they do."

room, and you looked to Him and asked Him how to pray: Would you then say to Him, "Thank you for your suggestion Lord"? Would you choose to see His worded reply as but an example of how to pray as many denominations teach? Would you take His saying, *"In this manner"* (as He does in Matthew's Gospel) as reason not to pray with Him these words of His answer to your question? Those who say it's recited only s a model of prayer are choosing to put their own spin on His words. They will quote Matt.6:6-7 and Phil.4:6-7 of how we must pray with heart, and not to do so with vain words as the heathen do. It's ludicrous in the least even to suggest that to recite these words to God, words that Christ recited Himself, as praying as the heathen do. Certainly true it is that any and all our prayer should be with a humbled and open heart, but this surely does not exclude the recital of the words Jesus spoke when asked how to pray.

It comes across to me, that being absent of His physical presence, and thus only the reading of His recited reply, some take a sort of arm-chair-like viewpoint towards these words coming from Christ; giving them rather a kind of least assessment, and as well in what manner they were meant.[28] It's not that they put His words down, but perceive them in a rather cavalier way.

Just think about it in this hyperbole way: Imagine how incredibly exalting, while yet how incredibly humbling, it would be to recite these very words with Jesus, the Lord of the universe, who so long ago spoke them.

---

[28] Of course this is not to mean it is the only way to pray.

The apostles sincerely sought from Christ His answer on this intimate and so important of a question of how to pray believing He would have an answer. He did. Why would anyone come to think it right to devalue the words of His answer to anything less than worthy of a frequent, humbled, and heartfelt recital?

With faith in Christ, let us slowly recite His answer.

"Our Father who art in heaven"
(edifying God's place in heaven and His fatherly love)

"hallowed be thy name"
(to have highest reverence of His very name)

"thy kingdom come, thy will be done,
on earth, as it is in heaven"
(our wanting and calling upon His will
to unite heaven and earth)

"give us this day our daily bread"
(requesting and acknowledging our dependence)

"forgive us our trespasses as we forgive
those who trespass against us"
(recognizing, and accepting, that He measure us
by the same manner and means that we use upon others)

and lead us not into temptation
but deliver us from evil.
(which He certainly does offer to the penitent)

That We

Be

one

The Matter of Authority

The matter of authority is divisive among the Christian faithful. It is truly the crux of all divisions amongst the many Christian faiths and its believers.

As we read in Matt.28:18, Jesus claims all authority, saying to His disciples ... *"All power is given unto me in heaven and in earth. Go ye therefore, and teach all nations, baptizing them in the name of the Father, and of the Son, and of the Holy Ghost: Teaching them to observe all things whatsoever I have commanded you."* If Christ is to be believed as having all authority in heaven and on earth, then in our *"believing"* in Him, we ought to accept His divine wisdom. That wisdom of His ought take into account having these men, His apostles and closest disciples, imperfect though they be, as His chosen human witnesses ... and to their having His delegated authority and the spiritual powers He bestowed upon them, to cast out demons; to heal the sick; to forgive sins; and to preach and teach the good news of salvation in Jesus Christ. Jesus said they would even do greater works than He did![29] Nevertheless, there

---

[29] John14:12 (This too is a statement by Christ that is hard to trust).

are those who aren't willing to accept that men, so ordained, can have such authority, never mind forgive sins. Look at it like this: Your boss gives you a gift for someone. He tells you that when it is asked for that you give it to them. So ... when it comes to be asked for and you give it; who gave it to them? You? Or your boss? In the direct sense, you did. But in the ultimate sense, this gift was given to them by your boss. It is by his authority that you gave this gift. Certainly, were there no boss, there would be no gift.

The ministry of the apostles began at first by their spoken word, and later in the writings of a few.[30] I take special note, that Jesus, upon the onset of their ministry, literally breathes on these disciples, saying, *"Receive ye the Holy Spirit"* [31] There can be no question that a very superior and extraordinary purpose it has for these disciples. These men, though not impeccable or without sin, are surely special, and must have a exceptional role in God's divine plan. Thus it is, that they received the Holy Spirit in this astounding of a manner (the only other time we read of God's doing this is in Genesis2:7, as He breathes life into Adam).

To then think that these most extra-ordinary men, these first stewards of the Gospel, these first teachers, knowing that they have been given the most important of all tasks in the world and in eternal life itself; these protectors of

---

[30] 1Cor2:10, 11:1-2; 2Cor2:9, 10:8; 2Thess3:4-6, 3:14; 1Tim4:11; Lk24:45; 2Pet1:20; Heb13:17
[31] John20:22

the faith, they who were breathed upon by Christ with the Holy Spirit, who were led to know all truth,[32] who were given tremendous authority and phenomenal spiritual powers by Christ (*"as my Father hath sent me, even so send I you"*), would they not deem it absolutely crucial to the continuance and protection of the faith to ordain successors of themselves with those same Christ-ordained gifts?[33] To think they did not just disparages plausible reasoning.

Indeed it is that throughout those early generations, as the church grew, the faith had to be protected by passing it on from the apostles, to the bishoprics, to the presbyters.[34] We read in the Scriptures of bishops being added; and even of a successor to the traitor, Judas, being chosen by the apostles.[35] If a successor was appointed of him, how can we think they would not have the prudence, as well as the authority, to ordain successors of themselves as they faced the inevitable consequences of their lives on earth coming to an end? And that this would continue throughout Christian history in the church, even to this day. It just stands to reason that they would do so, so as to maintain the functioning of the His Church in carrying on

---

[32] John16:13, 20:21; Mk.4:11   When others denied of them this God-ordained knowledge and authority, how might you say they should have responded?

[33] Luke9:1

[34] Thus it is that the faith began and spread without the New Testament Bible.

[35] Acts1:15-26, 14:23, 20-28; 1Thess.2:6-7, 1:1-2, 12; 1Cor.12:27-29; Eph.4:11, 2:20; 1Tim.3:1-8, 4:13-14, 5:17-22, 2:1-2

commissioned ministry which began especially upon the apostle Peter. A Church whose elders, both in its beginning and throughout its history, would so obviously know better than to be so negligent and irresponsible in allowing it to cease in its perpetual existence by their oversight in the ordaining of successors to themselves! If the role of the apostles was intended by our Lord to end with the original twelve, what need would there have been to fill the vacancy left by Judas? (yet, in Acts1 we see a definite, even somewhat urgent, need to fill the "office" of his apostleship). It is evidently of consequence to God for us to know that such successorship was passed on at the very onset of Christianity, and that it was ordained by those already having legitimate title to this office.

In the Scriptural writings of Peter and Paul it's unmistakable that they spoke and wrote of what they knew to be the truth of God, and did so with authority (having sacred knowledge, and spiritual powers, that Christ had bestowed upon and to them).[36] Consider the parable given by Christ in Mk.13:34 in speaking of Himself: *"For the Son of man is as a man taking a far journey, who left his house, and gave authority to his servants, and to every man his work, and commanded the porter to watch."*

As for the pope, well, there is no "pope" [37] mentioned in Scripture. For many a Protestant this is cause enough to

---

[36] Jn.14:12, 20:23, 2Cor.5:18, Jas.5:16, Acts1:20, Lk.10:16, 7:46

[37] His true title is "Bishop of Rome" (this church being the head of the Roman Catholic churches throughout the world).

dismiss any notion that there is a single human head of the Christian faith. As they see it, it's plain and simple: If something is not in the Bible, it just ain't so ... can't be so. No further reasoning would even be proper. Nevertheless, I'm going to present some:

Peter is mentioned in the New Testament 191 times.[38] Next is the apostle John, 48 times. When the names of *all* the apostles are listed, Peter is always first. Scripture sometimes simply speaks of him, and-the-rest-of-the-apostles. He's frequently shown as the spokesman amongst them. In Mt.16:13-20, Jesus speaks of Peter having gotten a direct revelation from the Father. Angels single Peter out amongst the apostles in Acts12:7. In Lk.24:33-35, the risen Christ appears first to Peter. In Acts1:15-26, it is Peter who leads the apostles in their selecting of a successor to Judas. In Acts2, it is Peter, who on his own, preaches to the crowd. In Acts3:12-16, it is Peter who is written of professing that his heavenly gift comes, not from him, but from Jesus Christ; in Acts3, it is Peter who performs the first miracle of an apostle; and in Acts9:33, he also performs the first miracle after the Pentecost; and yet another in Acts9:37-41, it is Peter who prays for a dead woman (whereby she came back to life). In Acts5:15, it is Peter to whom crowds are drawn. In Acts10:33-48, he is the one to receive the revelation from God that the Gentiles are to be welcomed into the faith without being circumcised and subject to the Jewish law. In Acts15:1-7, it is Peter who speaks up amongst the council of elders who were in disagreement and

---

[38] As Peter, Simon Peter, Simon, and Cephas.

argument over this matter ... and it is Peter who settles it once and for all. And in Gal.2:11-14, we read of Paul rebuking Peter; showing that he, though chief among them, is not faultless, nor is he unapproachable.[39]

It is to Peter exclusively, that Christ says to him that upon this rock He [Christ] will build His church, and will give to Peter the keys of the kingdom of heaven. It is well recognized that there is contention of the meaning of this to the Protestants, saying that Peter is not the rock: "Christ is the rock!" they insist. By this, I take it, is meant that Jesus is the cornerstone of the church. Well, that's for sure! If Peter is taken as "the rock" (as the Catholic church does), it is as the human head of the church. There's no differing consequence for these words of Christ to Peter whether you take Peter to be the rock or a pebble; it is upon Peter whom Christ says He will build His Church whom He now knows to be solid in his faith. Christ does not build "His Church" upon John, or Matthew, Phillip, or either James', Luke, or Mark, Andrew, or Bartholomew, Thomas, or Judas, or anyone else. He builds His Church upon Peter. [40] Who can differ with this? I mean look: If I say directly to you, and only to you, that I'll be leaving, and upon you I will be starting my new company, would it not be obvious that this means you're then to be in charge of this company ... and not anyone else who might later come along?

---

[39] Pope Francis says of himself, "I am a sinner". Nothing special about this, but many non-Catholics believe no Pope would ever say it
[40] Mt.16:18-19 (nor to Martin Luther).

In choosing Peter as He did for this ordained and sacred assignment, Christ has placed an astounding trust in him (notwithstanding that he was referred to as Satan by Christ, and how it is that Peter denied Him during His arrest, and perhaps because he denied Him, and been forgiven, that Peter had come, all the more so, to have a deepened loyalty to Jesus that is, well, rock-solid). Whatever the reason, Peter is the one chosen to be in command of the church that Christ initiated upon His departure, and as Christ put it, to feed His sheep (Jn.21:17).

Consider too, the serious and most solemn implication of Christ telling Peter, and again exclusively Peter, not only that upon him will He begin His church, but that what he, Peter, binds on earth will be bound in heaven, and what he shall loose on earth will be loosed in heaven.[41] *"Wow!"* If it weren't coming from the lips of Christ, I could only see it as completely non-sensical. It's so incredible a thing for He who has all authority on earth and in the heavens, to then grant to this mortal, imperfect, man. But He did.

For the Protestants and Baptists though, there is no *" Wow!"* here of what Jesus just said and, thus, initiated by His instructions to Peter. Instead, there is denial that Peter is to be in charge of His church as it's human head and, thus, of the Christian faithful. Such a profound statement made to Peter, *that what he loosens or binds on earth will be so done in heaven,* doesn't really mean

---

[41] Mt.18:18

all that much as they see it. Their cavalier way of looking at it is itself a "*Wow*" to me.

Now, as is well known, the idea of human authority and infallibility is vehemently rejected by non-Catholics. Yet it's taken for granted of the apostles, who though not perfect nor without sin, wrote Scripture we believe is without error and is sacred.

Yet too, and this is ironic really, that in seeking a denomination, there is, in consequence, not one authority, but everyone sees themselves as their own authority.

Let me describe: In search for church affiliation, many shop around. This is done by a pick-and-choose process ... joining, as they will, the denomination that is the most similar to their self-held beliefs and style, and many quite naturally choosing what they've grown up with, and are thus comfortable with. This is to be expected of us. Nonetheless, and speaking in a most general way of course, if for instance, they believe that abortion is a matter of one's personal decision, they seek a church that teaches accordingly (Presbyterian); If they prefer a church that is democratic, whereby the congregation gets to vote on doctrinal beliefs and matters of morality, they join the Congregational church; if they rather want one that is emotive, waves their arms high in praise to God, and believe they speak in tongues, then they join the Pentecostal sect of Protestantism; if they believe that gambling or the drinking of alcohol is to be avoided, they seek the church that teaches this (most Baptist); if they don't believe that infants should be baptized, they shun any denomination that does so;[42] some especially enjoy a church with good music and choir, and perhaps a pastor that sings; others are particularly appreciative of a humble pastor ("don't call me reverend kind of person"); yet others seek a church with a dynamic and charismatic preacher who has a way of persuading people to his (or her) altar call;[43] some choose a church that is entertaining (a good band and singers); for others, a church that has a close camaraderie amongst the parishioners is particularly to their liking, that welcomes them and their family into the congregation in the sharing of their Christian fellowship; as well there are those that seek a church community of their own ethnicity: while those with children may specifically look for a church having good programs that will involve them in various ways (the children and teenagers especially have a liking for this); some will simply go along with their spouse's choice giving little consideration to doctrines espoused; then there are those denominations where, for the most part, you pretty much need to be born into them, as with the Amish and Mennonites; now should one want a church that caters a bit more to the

---

[42] By the faith of their parents, in accord with God's commandment to Moses, eight-day old boys, though they cannot decide nor act on their own, are presented to God for the infant to thus receive God's covenant upon them (Gen.17:9-14). So too, by the faith of their parents, are infants baptized. (Mt.19:13-14, Mk.10:13-14, Lk.18:16).

QUESTION: Is Baptism merely symbolic? Acts2:38, Rom.6:3-4, Lk.18:15-17, 1Pet.3:18-21, Col.2:11-14, Tit.3:5 ... these Scriptures put forth evidence that is quite compelling otherwise.

[43] A good Protestant tradition.

"free thinker" in all of us, and has an all-encompassing view of other faiths, then the Unitarian church is just the place; Some people, attempting to be all-caring, or all-non-offending, or simply unwilling to scrutinize for the truth, will say it doesn't matter much which denomination one is in, as they are all serving God in their own fashion; and finally, if one doesn't quite like any that are around, they might even start their own brand new denomination.

Thus each person has their own reasons, with some even placing doctrine secondary to their personal reasons, or choosing their doctrine-of-truth as they see it. Some pastors are supportive of this autonomy in saying to their parishioners, that if they feel differently than what is preached, they are then to read their Bibles at home and believe accordingly as the Holy Spirit may guide them. Yet this is clearly in violation of God's word that Scripture is not to be of one's private interpretation.[44]

Certainly many of these denominations have much to be admired. The Amish, for instance, live a life of simplicity that deserves to be well-regarded, and the various considerations mentioned here of one's personal needs do have worth. But having as the first priority for choosing one's very faith-belief in any of these ways, is to give license to one's own self as being the final arbiter of truth, and so too, to avoid sincere scrutiny of those teachings that don't make them "feel" good. Thus, their questions for choosing a denomination or a particular church are: "Do I like what they offer?" "Are they

---

[44] 2Peter1:20

friendly and welcoming?" "Do I like the sermons?" Indeed it is, I've come to notice that the sermon, that is the pastor's speaking ability and presentation, and his personality, are often a most influencing reason in the choosing of which church to attend. Some might say, "He's on fire for the Lord!" and other such comments regarding the pastor and thus the church that's chosen.

As for individual autonomy in choosing a denomination, it is an attractive and seemingly agreeable attribute to most of us (we all like autonomy), but I ask ever sincerely, is the wanting of such self-determination and spiritual independence a giving in to one's pride? Are we to be in charge of what a church is to teach us as the truth, or is the church to be in charge of what it teaches?

Often it is said by non-Catholic fellow Christians, that we ought not to seek the truth in any institution or religion. Scripture, they point out, says that Jesus alone saves. This is indeed so, as Christ elaborates in the Gospels, and later also by the apostles in their writings. For sure, the Catholic revelation of this truth embraces fully that salvation is by Christ alone. In doing so it takes into account all instructions given by Christ, with the most imperative of all being given to the apostles. Jesus makes it quite clear that He has placed these chosen men to have charge of the spreading the Gospel truth, and that they can, and that they must, do so with full authority. He even says to them: *"He that heareth you heareth me:*

and he that despiseth you despiseth Him that sent me." [45]

How very evident it is that this would be in opposition to what Christ wants and established with these closest of His disciples. That we are to listen to them and follow what they say is true. Not our own concepts (I know this is not especially comforting to our wanting a sense of autonomy).

Jesus commissioned these particular men, and gave only to them, authority in the spreading of the Gospel. To proclaim, "Christ and only Christ", we've really got to encompass all of Christ. If we say, "Christ and only Christ", while excluding what Christ proclaims, are we not then minimizing our faith in Christ by dismissing some portions of what He says?

Christ makes it so very clear that there are those to whom we are obliged to trust and obey for they have a teaching authority that He gave them. We're not offered a choice by Christ whether to believe those He has so ordained, or to not accept their authority ... to not do so, is to not accept His authority. [46] Whether we like what they say, or are uncomforted by what they say and proclaim, we are obliged to follow their teachings, not our own, as to what is the truth of the Gospel.

We certainly do read that Peter and Paul gave commands in their writings, and as they themselves

---

[45] Luke10:16; (envision someone saying to them that they go directly to Christ).

[46] Luke10:16 Note, that others could spread the Gospel, but only they had the final say of what was Truth and what was not.

write, some were conveyed verbally face-to-face.[47] Certainly to refute Paul's teachings and commands, by word or letter, is to refute Christ; indeed to despise Peter or Paul, as well as the other apostles, is to despise Christ, and the Father as well. So says Christ.

Unexpected indeed it would be for those with this teaching authority to now be absent within the Body-of-Christ ... as if of days gone by.

In essence, the teaching that it is Christ-and-only-Christ, is a false teaching, in so far as it is incomplete ... for Christ says plain as day, that there are men commissioned by Him with authority whom we ought not reject. So it's not Christ-and-only-Christ, for it is they too. If this was so in the past, is it no longer so?

Though it may sound as if someone is so, so profoundly dedicated to Christ, by declaring over, and over, and over, and over from the pulpit, "Christ-and-only-Christ" ... "Christ-and-only-Christ" ... "Christ-and-only-Christ" (as I once heard a Baptist pastor do), it simply is not the full truth when indeed what is being ignored is that a religion with an organized hierarchy of bishops, of priests (known then as presbyters), deacons, and others, was established by the apostles shortly after the onset of His Church, so as to assign different task as was needed by the growing church.[48]

---

[47] 1Thess.4:2, 1John2:3, 3:24, 5:2, 1Cor11:1 (be followers of Paul), 1Tim4:11. In 2Cor.2:9, Paul insist that they are to be obedient. (not the kind of command most of us like).

[48] Romans12:4-8; 1Cor.12:12/27; Col.1:24; 1Pet.5:1

Unexpected as well would it be for such to now be gone within the Body-of-Christ as is so within the Baptist's religions and many of the Protestant's too. Yet this is what many of the Protestant and Baptists faiths want us to accept as so.

Be most mindful that those who would tell us "all you need is Christ", as they overlook all-that-is-Christ, are not speaking the fullness of the Christian faith.[49]

Just imagine saying to Peter or Paul (or any of the apostles for that matter) that you don't accept their teaching authority ... for you go directly to Christ? Or that you interpret a Scripture, a doctrine, or a moral teaching differently than what they are telling you. Or suppose an Israelite were to say, "I don't want to listen to Moses, Lord, he's much to slow, I only listen to you." (that person surely would then have remained a slave in Egypt).

Indeed God has always used human leaders to establish His relationships and thus to bring to people His proclamations and commandments. Think on this: Is it not incomprehensible that now, in our present time, the sacred faith of Christianity, which at its onset had trusted human authority, would become absent of trusted authority today? How could Christianity have changed like this? Could you accept that this is now so ... that it's a credible consequence of time in accord with God's will upon the spreading of the Gospel to all nations as He so instructed?

---

[49] Mk.9:7 (*This is my beloved Son: Hear ye Him*).

It would be as if we now have a different form of Christianity; a different means of its functioning; and whereby in the earliest days you could trust in a Scriptural, doctrinal, and moral teaching authority, but not any more[50] (the old way is replaced by a new way).

Thanks be to God ... for the Catholic is trusting Christ by trusting His words and commandments. This is so crucial in our trust of Christ, for in so doing we trust the teaching authority of the church because Christ ordained it. The Mass is far beyond a pastor's sermon (no matter how good it may be), for the Mass is a reverent worship service; it is a sacrificial service devoted to the one-time sacrifice of Christ where in His last Passover supper, He spoke of His offering us His body and His blood that we may have life and be truly united with Him in a most down-to-earth manner that goes so far beyond words. The Mass is, in all its humility, devoted in faith to this commandment of Christ: "Take, eat, this is my body ..."

In the Mass we publicly proclaim our sinfulness and our need for the forgiveness of Christ; and ask for prayer from one another. As members in the one-Body-of-Christ, we ask also for the prayers and intercession of those in heaven, for the Body-of-Christ includes all who live in Christ, here on earth and those in heaven.[51]

---

[50] 1Tim.3:15 The pillar and ground of truth *is the church* ; 2Tim.4:2-5 "*...For the time will come when they will not endure sound doctrine [...] And they shall turn away their ears from the truth.*

[51] Indeed there is not one Body-of-Christ here on earth and yet another Body of Christ in heaven. Romans 8:38-39, Eph.4:4, 6:18, 1Tim.2:1

That We

Be

one

$$*{*}*{*}*{*}*{*}*{*}*{*}*$$

The Matter of One Church

If Christ is to be believed as having all authority, then we, in faith, ought to believe in His words to Peter; for clearly they are upon him that Christ begins His church. Christ, the Savior of the world, started His church in this way, because He wanted there to be one. He didn't do so for it to be an obstacle, or a hindrance to man ... nor for it to ever fail.

Upon His departure, Christ gives to His disciples, that is only to His closest disciples, *all knowledge and truth,* that they may teach the truth, and do so with an authority that is absolute, and exclusively theirs: That they may, thus, confidently promote and be protectors of the faith (and later to come, the Scriptures). It is consequently they, and only they, who may identify and call what is heresy, "heresy"; and do so because of the knowledge of the truth which Christ bestowed to them in so special and exclusive of a way.[52]

This is a crucial teaching in Scripture as I certainly see it. So, let me repeat it a bit differently: Christ, by these instructions to these disciples, instituted a human

---

[52] Lk.24:45;

hierarchy, who had more spiritual knowledge than all others; who had sole authority to protect the faith; and who could inform others of the truth, in a way that they could not inform themselves. This is not to say they, and ourselves, cannot ask for guidance from the Holy Spirit (for of course anyone can and should), but that even in doing so, the faithful are to remain subject to the teaching and guidance of those to whom Christ gave authority, otherwise it becomes a free-for-all.

It is Jesus who promised to send to the apostles the Holy Spirit to guide His church into all truth, and to be with them and His church so instituted till the end of time; telling them that the powers of evil would not ever, ever prevail against His church.[53]

So what then? Are we to even consider that Jesus didn't accomplish this? That He failed in what He promised, which resulted in the church He initiated and instructed falling into irreparable error and corruption, only to be rescued by the reformers some fifteen hundred years later (who had even been using an inferior Bible for all that time until the corrected 'King James' version was then adopted)?[54] (footnote here gives interesting info on King James).

---

[53] John1:13; Mt.28:20; Acts2:47; Mk.13:34; Mt.16:18

[54] King James was the king of Scotland and England in the early 1600's. In this time period, he sponsored a translation of the Bible which came to be named after him. He was as well a poet and writer, most notable for his book titled: *'The True Law of Free Monarchies',* in which he argued that there is a theological basis for monarchy. He writes of the divine right of kings, explaining that, for Biblical reasons, kings are higher beings than other men.

As it is claimed by Protestants that the King James Bible is the truest Bible, this then says that the Bible that was in use for well over a thousand years (this would be the Catholic one Martin Luther had prior to his departure from the Catholic faith) was flawed, and was subsequently "corrected" by him in some way? Yet to do so, beyond mere translational, would be defiant of John's words of warning in his book of Revelations that there be nothing added or removed. But Luther must have changed it to replace the faulty one, or it could not then have become a "truer" Bible.

From what I understand, history records that the reformers sought the earliest Scriptures from which to translate (those would of course be the ones that were in the earlier Bibles), seeking (I believe sincerely) to do so accurately. Nonetheless, initiated as it is some 1600 years after the Christian faith had been in existence, it remains, that they could only take this kind of action by claiming their own authority, and believing in their own competence to do so, I trust, without error (infallibility).

Speaking of the Bible (again to say, the Catholic one that Martin Luther had been using) ... how and who decided which books in the New Testament were the ones to be selected those many hundreds of years after Christ? Did God just drop the New Testament all complete with the twenty seven manuscripts in it from heaven? Well, of course not ... so then there had to be humans involved. Seeing as Martin Luther initially had a Catholic Bible ... it then follows that it must have been the Catholic church which scrutinized and grappled with the strivings of which writings they believed to be sacred, and should thus be included, and which should not (there were many to consider).

Thus it is, that here, unknowingly by many, the authority of the Catholic church, is not only accepted, but revered ... for it is believed the task of selecting the 27 books that are now in the New Testament was accomplished, without error (infallibly), by this group and council of Catholics (this does not mean that they were impeccable or without sin). [55]

Billy Graham, a prominent and internationally esteemed Protestant minister, wrote in his book, 'Peace With God':[56] "The important thing is not how we do it [drawing closer to God], but the sincerity and depth of purpose with which we do it, and we should each find and join the church in which as individuals we can best accomplish this."

---

[55] Critics dismiss the role of the Catholic councils that were convened in 393-397 in selecting the books of the New Testament ... contending, I suppose, that the Holy Spirit caused the 27 books to somehow just fall into place on their own. They would have us believe that these councils that dealt with them were nothing more than bishops getting together to say "Wow, look at that!"

[56] Pages 223 & 225. May the good Lord bless Billy Graham. He has done so much to initiate many people to the faith, along with helping people in need throughout the world. (NOTE: The concept of an invisible church having a mystical-body-of-dispersed true-believers is a Baptist and Protestant tradition. It certainly explains away the divisions amongst the denominations as being of no real consequence for the truly faithful exist within them all).

Paul says:[57] *"Now I beseech you brethren by the name of our Lord Jesus Christ, that ye all speak the same thing, and that there be no divisions among you; but that ye be perfectly joined together in the same mind, and in the same judgment."*

Pastor Graham says: "Now that you have accepted Christ as your Savior...you have already become a member of the great church invisible." He goes on to write: "The New Testament teaches that while there is actually one universal church there can be any number of local churches formed into various denominations and societies or councils."

Paul writes: *"There is one Lord, and one faith."* [58]

So much so does our Lord Jesus Christ want for us to be one, that sacred Scripture quotes Him praying to the Father, *"That they all may be one; as thou, Father, art in me, and I in thee, that they also may be one in us: that the world may believe that thou hast sent me."* [59] Accordingly unity should be of vital concern to us. Any church made up of Spirit-filled people ought to be consumed of heart by this prayer of Christ, and the commands of the apostles, that we be of one accord. We are a family. We are a family that is, sad to say, separated by our Scriptural and doctrinal differences (nor need we think globally, as this is so even within our personal families, friends, and others close to us).

---

[57] 1Cor.1:10, 11-12; Note also ... 2Cor.13:11
[58] Eph.4:5
[59] John17:21

We are not one.

For Baptists and Protestants in general, it sure seems it is compulsory to discredit the Catholic church. Just about every time I listen on radio or TV to one or the other, they don't only present their faith as they see it, but so often they just gotta throw in something or other about how the Catholics have it wrong!

There is a serious inconsistency in any denomination claiming to be Spirit-led, while fostering disunity in the Christian family.[60] Christianity today is experiencing, again in its history, many attacks upon the faith. There are persecutions throughout many of the world's nations (some so very severe involving torture and death). Me? What do I know about suffering for my faith? I sit here on a comfortable chair as I type at the computer writing of this. I've just had a good left-over dinner, and am enjoying a hot cup of Dunkin Donuts coffee, while at this very moment there are tens-of-thousands of minority faiths in fear for their lives atop a mountain in Iraq; they're surrounded by religious zealots who seek to impose their beliefs by threat of torture and death. Some are dying of thirst and exhaustion but dare not come down; so too hundreds of young women have been abducted there, to God only knows what fate; and I hear of hundreds of men, women, and children burned alive or beheaded if they will not denounce their faith (Christian or otherwise). As they suffer in fear and

---

[60] John15:17

suppression, in contrast, what a God-given freedom we have to speak openly to one another about our faiths and beliefs.

Let's use this freedom.

Let's insist on this freedom, for even in America, the land of the free, the government is more and more coming to trespass upon the religious liberties of its citizens. There's government suppression in the very mentioning of Christ in our public schools. Even in our universities! Secularism is turning out to be the mainstream in our culture, and has become hostile to matters of faith in any public role ... persuading many of our young, who are easily led, to look down upon matters of Christian belief and faith;

Christianity is, thus, faced with matters of very somber consequence. Our dwindling congregations, and an ever increasing antagonism against Christian morality (of which I myself sorely contributed), along with a cultural denial of an eternal heaven and hell, or of mankind's need of salvation, has brought about trials and challenges for all of Christianity everywhere in the world. Self-exalting-pride and sin go unrestrained and are even praised in our society and media. Our world, a world so beautiful in many, many ways, is yet sinking spiritually downward, in our wars, gross atrocities, and individual brutalities. So too within our very culture here in America (and elsewhere), views opposing Christian morality are being extolled by an "enlightened secularism" as being for the good of humanity by those having a misguided compassion that is supportive of many of our sinful behaviors and ways. Love that seeks to speak of sin is condemned as intolerant, hateful and phobic in one way or another. Any mention of there being "a truth" is labeled as narrow-mindedness, self-righteous, and in the least, old fashioned ... while running round and round the altar of money, possessions, or fame seeking happiness, some of us run round the altar of power hoping for fulfillment; while some of us crave after pleasures, becoming in time enslaved to sexual gratifications, or alcohol and drugs ... all is to no avail.

The cause for freedom to many, especially in the secular culture, is seen as accepting that everyone may, more or less, do their own thing. You know, "just be yourself", for no one ought to tell you how to live your life, is how its seen.

To enlighten this way of thinking, the true Christian compassion and message of love, mercy, and the need of salvation as sinners, is so, so much the better to be realized by our being unified.

Christ, upon His departure from earth, left us with a church (a Baptist pastor I know said this is heresy); yet I ask you, is it not obvious that Christ left us with a church upon His earthly departure when He said to Peter that He would start His church upon him? And that the apostles, filled with the Holy Spirit at Pentecost, were, by the commission of Christ, to be administers of His church with full authority. No power of evil, said Jesus, would prevail against this church (and there has been much both externally and from within throughout its history; and very shamefully has it been so within even in our present time). And just as Christ said it would, the church has prevailed ... and its mandated mission, to spread the revelation of God's love and salvation to all nations, continues on now into its third millennium.[61] No one, and nothing, within or without, can ever withdraw or discontinue the church in this mission ... for, by God, the church is willed and led by the Holy Spirit. How so? Because Christ said it would be.

Baptists along with many Protestant denominations, are taught of the Catholic church as being a false church. Their very doctrines are defined to a certain degree by their being in protest of the Catholic church; it's drilled into them to "be against the Catholic church"; that its teachings are un-Scriptural, that Catholics are idolatrous, and of their having vain-traditions-of-men (to name but a very, very few).

These anti-Catholic descriptions and pronouncements, I've found, are accepted pretty much unquestioningly. Bible Scriptures are learned and memorized, and even at a very young age they do so quite well.[62] They are told by their pastors that their teachings come from "the authoritative word of God", and will state that "Christ is sufficient" is to mean that nothing at all else is needed, or wanted, in regards to one's salvation. I'll tell yah, when I

---

[61] Mt.16:18-19

[62] Even seven year olds, I have witnessed will know where in the Bible is any particular book. Impressive indeed! God bless 'em.

63

was personally challenged by being asked, "Are you saying that Christ is not sufficient?" it made me gulp! "How could I respond to this?" My words of retort at the time were not at all clearly expressed. I mean, what could I say? That Christ is not sufficient? That seemed so incongruous! I felt so inept.

Now ... given some time to reflect on this conviction, that *"Christ is sufficient"*, as it is used by Protestants and Baptists in refuting the church and it's sacraments, I begin by examining what one means here of "Christ": If "Christ" is to mean only-the-divine-person-Jesus, then the statement is incomplete, for there's then a separation of the person-Christ, from the words-and-deeds of Christ. On the other hand, if by the use of "Christ" is to mean *all* that Christ is: that is, His-divine-person-along with-all-His-authority, and all-His-teachings, and all-His-instructions, and all-His-deeds-and-His-commands ... then the statement is true. To say this conversely, the separating of Christ from His words and deeds, is to split Him apart from all that He is. It is only *Christ-in-all-his-totality* that is sufficient. This distinction is decisive.

This means that when Christ says this bread is my body, and to eat it in remembrance of Him, then accepting the bread as His body, true and present, and doing so as He commanded, is a part of His sufficiency; when He says to Peter that He will start His church upon him, then that church becomes a part of the sufficiency of Christ.

As for such dangers as idolatry, un-Scriptural teachings, and any artificial impediments to Christ and salvation, certainly do need and deserve thorough examination. Such discussions ought not to become a quarrel. But I've noticed there being an avoidance of anything Catholic by many a Baptist/Protestant, rather than any heartfelt discussion. It's like "catholic" (though it simply means 'universal' in Greek) is a foul word; and many come to accepting and passing on whatever anti-Catholic teachings that they come to hear; while failing to notice, or perhaps avoiding, Scriptural verses that bring any possible credence to Catholic church teachings (even to have EWTN on in their presence is bothersome to some I've found). I know for myself, when asked something about the Catholic faith, it's not uncommon that it's with a suggestion of mockery.

To know Christ, to have a personal relation with Christ, is a lifetime quest ... in His love for us we have visible signs and down-to-earth means instituted by Him to give grace. These are the sacraments of the Catholic church. Written of in the Scriptures, the gifts of the sacraments act to progress throughout our lives, His most literal and tangible closeness with us, our knowing of Him, and He of us, especially in the Eucharist and as well as we reveal all of our self to Him in the confessional.[63] Indeed, that's a really personal relationship with the Lord!

Ever since the Protestant revolt in the 16th century, the

---

[63] THE SEVEN SACRAMENTS ARE: Baptism – Jn.3:5, Rom.6:4
Reconciliation – Jn.20:23;   Confirmation - Jn.20:21-23
The Eucharist - Jn.6:51-58;   Holy Ordination - Cor.11:23-25
Matrimony – Matt..9:4-6   Anointing of the sick - Jas.5:14

church has been accused by some of ignoring, opposing, hiding, and even destroying the Bible to keep it from the people. It's condemningly said that Bibles were chained by the church to the walls so that people could not take them home to read during the Middle Ages. And the church, they say, refused to translate the Bible into the language of the common people in order to hinder personal reading.[64] Even, they say, the Church was so diabolical as to burn 'em!

When examining such charges against this "false" church, consider this: First off, if the church truly wanted to destroy the Bible, why would her monks have worked so diligently and meticulously through the early centuries making copies? Before the printing press, copies of the Bible were hand written with unrelenting and so painstaking an accuracy. Oh yes, Bibles were chained! Chained to the walls of churches they were, because each copy was precious both spiritually and materially. It took a monk a year, I read, to hand copy the entire Bible (with just one Bible requiring skins from about 300 sheep). So Bibles were scarce and expensive. The chaining of them kept them safe from damage or theft, so all the people could benefit from them.

And oh yes indeed! The church burned Bibles! She did so to prohibit the dissemination of rogue Bibles, or those printed with errors, in order to preserve the integrity of Holy Scripture. This action was necessary if the church

---

[64] Latin was the prominent language of those educated; most people could not read (thus artworks were used to present the Gospel).

was, and is, to be the protector of the Gospels. Does this action make the church anti-Bible? Of course not. If the Catholic church truly wanted to destroy the Bible, she had ample opportunity to do so within the first thousand years.[65]

To put it mildly, these kinds of charges are frivolous. There are sincere concerns and questions of the doctrines and faith of the Catholic church by non-Catholics; and they are deserving of thoughtful response and answers.[66] Quite often, aversions to the Catholic faith are due more to misunderstanding, or the secular media. As well, some are due to not making any real, honest-to-God effort in seeking out the church's Scriptural justifications and illumination of its teachings ... *for they certainly do exist.*

The seeking of a wanted outcome in one's search for the truth of a matter won't cut it. The seeking of truth needs to be earnest of heart, and as well with the God-given ability of sound reasoning. If little effort is put into it, our conscience can become numbed in heart and mind. Indeed, we seek the help of the Holy Spirit, but to then think that each of us are unequivocally self-possessed in receiving the truth, without the express ordination from Christ, is quite less than humble, I'd say. That this self-possession of truth isn't so is glaringly evident in the

---

[65] Peter, in his second epistle (3:16), warns that Scripture can be distorted to one's own destruction (evidently proper interpretation of Scripture ought not to be taken for granted).

[66] There are so many, I'll not get into all of them here; and as well, some require much elaboration or considerable Scriptural exegesis, and I am limited to do so.

multiplicity of interpretations on the Scriptures (and this by sincerely meaning people wanting the truth).

The Catholic church is deeply devoted to Christ as the one and only mediator between God and man. By its Christ-instituted sacraments, the church is mystical, she is compassionate, in a tangible way, of God's consoling and patient mercy; and by its long history of prayerful study of the Scriptures passed on for nearly two-thousand years, she is full of spiritual wisdom; and is eager to thoughtfully explain her faith and mission as commissioned and protected by Christ. The church, in doing so, is not given to an imposing or condescending manner (as I may, sorry to say, be at times) ... but rather she does so in surrender to the ways and guidance of Christ. As the church is administered by humans, she has not been and is not perfect in this ... as she grows in understanding, and learning, however unfortunate at times, from her errors.

The church guides us to avoid being tossed to and fro by every wind of doctrine proposed by someone (and there are so, so, so many); thus helping us not to swerve from the truth about the revelation of Christ, and the redemption offered to mankind ... and in those most difficult of questions that do arise, to guide us that we may attain the truth with certainty.

In no way is the church "above" the Bible, as some accuse. It can, and does, explain, in a meaningful and Scriptural way, its doctrines, its sacraments, its relics, its statues, its bells, its candles, its incense, its rituals, its traditions, its prayers, its art, and its architectures.

Consider, if you will, the chains that Peter was held with when imprisoned. Might they have been kept by the early Christians? If so how would you want them to be treated? Would you want them to be saved, even treasured, and encased perhaps in a protective environment? Perhaps on display in a church? What of the shroud-of-Turin, even though its authenticity is inconclusive at this time, would you want it nevertheless treasured as if it is sacred (just in case); or would you have it treated merely as a piece of cloth until such time that we know conclusively?[67] What if the basket that the baby Moses was laid in and sent down the river were in our possession? Would you consider any of these items to be sacred and cherished in some special way? (do note, in Ex.13:19, Moses keeps a relic of the bones of Joseph). How about a statue or painting of an apostle ... is this not a means to reveal a bit of the Gospel story in a visual way? In Ex.20, only images *for-the-purpose-of-idolatry* does God forbid. In Dt.7:25, God denounces images made to their *false* gods. In 1Kings6:23-28, Solomon makes cherubim; In Ex.25:18 God Himself commands Moses to make statues of cherubim. These are man-made images, but they're not graven ones. How about statues or paintings of exemplary people, presidents, and others, is looking upon them with esteem idolatrous? What of personal relics? Is it idolatrous to deeply appreciate the relic of a loved one ... such as having a toy or hair-lock of a deceased child on a mantle,

---

[67] As may come to be when scientific means have progressed sufficiently to make such a determination.

or holding it in your hand as you in loving memory think of him or her?

Having been to many Baptist churches, I see how they are, for the most part, without ritual, and without art, pictures, and statues - ok. They say such things are graven images, and want especially that all focus be on Christ. Now wait a minute! Would they want to have their grandmother's home to be without photos of loved ones, both past and present in the family, and barren of art and other nice things? If her home were not barren in this way, would your love then be distracted away from her? Might having family photos, etc. even supplement your love for her? If so, why deem it wrong, or distracting, to adorn the Lord's house with icons of Christian history and people?

These first disciples were Jewish, and some of their preaching of Christ as the Messiah occurred in the Jewish temples.[68] Indeed, Jesus acclaims the sacredness of the Jewish Temple itself, by referring to it as: *"My house"... "My Father's house".*[69] Certainly the disciples would continue their ritual worship with a greater fervor to include now Christ as Messiah, for He fulfilled their Jewish faith. How can we make a blanket statement that religious ritual is wrong, when Christ Himself repeatedly partook in religious rituals? By His life-long participation

---

[68] The Jews who did not accept that Christ was the promised Messiah pushed them out of the temple, thus they also met in their homes (so too when ruling kings persecuted them).
[69] Mt.21:13, Mk.11:17, Jn.2:16

Christ sanctified those rituals as sacred.[70] His comments are not denouncing rituals, but only those who are insincere in their ways with them, and thus vain; be it in their rituals or in their prayers. The rituals of the Mass are not vain for they were instituted By Christ when He said, *"This is my body"* and *"This is my blood," "Do this in remembrance of me;"* and are as well the execution of those told of in John's Revelations.[71]

There is truly a boundless spiritual beauty and deepest of Christian mysteries that awaits you in the faith that is catholic should you sincerely seek to understand it. And should you grasp this truth, you will not abandon your faith in Christ ... you will be deepening and fulfilling your faith and your trust in Christ. You will open your heart to a worship that is so wrenching, for you will experience His love and mercy in a manner that is tangible. You will find peace of mind and heart that is deeply consoling, for it is down-to-earth ... just as Christ came down to earth as a man, that humanity could experience Him, and God's redeeming love, in this substantial and perceptible a way.

G. K. Chesterton, an internationally renowned writer, historian, theologist, and philosopher (once of the Unitarian faith), wrote of his inquisitive look into the church in a most interesting and honest a manner:[72]

---

[70] Mt.5:17, Acts21:28, Rom.3:31 (it is *vain* traditions, only vain and worthless traditions, which He condemned).

[71] Matt.26:26, 26:28, Rev. 6:9, 7:3, 4:8, 5:8, 15:16, 1:12 Indeed, how can ritual be wrong when you read of this in Scripture?

[72] 'The Catholic Church and Conversion' (minor paraphrasing); Used by permission: Ignatius Press *Works of G.K. Chesterton, Vol. 3*

The potential convert takes his first step rather unwittingly when he decides he's going to be fair to the Catholic Church. He does not think the Roman religion is true, but for the first time, he also doesn't think that the accusations against the Church are true. This important first step leads to a long and enjoyable second step, which is the utter fascination of learning what the Catholic Church really does teach. It is like discovering a new continent full of strange flowers and fantastic animals, which is at once wild and hospitable. But then the convert suddenly realizes with a shock that he can no longer be detached and impartial about the Catholic Church ... and the moment a man ceases to pull against it he feels a tug towards it. The moment he ceases to shout it down, he begins to listen to it with pleasure. The moment he tries to be fair to it he begins to be fond of it.

We do not really need a religion that is right where we are right [he says]. What we need is a religion that is right where we are wrong.

Now ... back to an example of seeking-the-truth-one-wants: A Baptist pastor handed me a list of his research studies which he says point the finger at Catholic teachings that are contrary to God's written Word; or whereby the church simply invented their doctrinal belief. For instance, in it he mentions how the church introduced, only in the year 1215, its belief in the transubstantiation of the bread and wine becoming the body and blood of Christ. What though he failed to find, had he sought any explanation from the church itself, would be that some were debating such a belief. To address this matter, a council of elders was, thus, assembled (just as the apostles did in Acts15:1-7), and the belief in transubstantiation, *a belief that had already been in practice,* was then affirmed, in writing, so that there be no ambiguity. So too, he sites prayer for the dead being established as of A.D. 330. It too was already in practice, and was given written affirmation at this time.

As previously mentioned in Acts 9:37-41, Peter knelt before a dead woman, and prayed for her. She was dead! The written word of God says she died. Not sick. Not in a coma. Dead. And Peter, not knowing of course how it would turn out, chose to pray for her.[73] How? How! (*I am so beside myself here!*), just how can anyone hold fast to believing it is erroneous to pray for the dead, when one of the blessed apostles did so, and God made it a point to let us know of it?[74]

What if, as Peter is about to pray for this dead woman, you who believe it is wrong to pray for the dead, were

---

[73] Acts9:37-40; Rom.8:38-39 (Peter, being but a man, he wouldn't know what his prayer would bring about, but only that it was quite ok to do so).

[74] So too do they pray for the dead in the Jewish faith. Are we to believe that this was never done while Jesus was an active member and participant in this way of the Jewish faith? We know too that Jesus speaks of saving the dead at some later time (Jn.5:25), and even brought some back to life (doesn't seem then they could have been consigned immediately upon their death to heaven or to hell).

there, and you tell him he shouldn't pray for her, and Peter believes in your spiritual knowledge, and follows it? Just look how this would have then changed this Biblical account of his prayer and its message to us from God.

Certainly to pray for someone who is dead would be aimless if the person is *at once* in heaven or in hell. Evident it is, that Peter did not believe this; and being but a mortal and imperfect man, just as with us, it would have been aimless for him to do so. How apparent it is that this is not the case for there could not be one truth then that is now not a truth today. I say again, the scriptural account of Peter's prayer here, it's meaning and purpose, had he listened, would be decidedly altered for all time by this person who told him not to. So what and who are we to believe then? He who says not to pray for the dead, or with Peter who did? [75]

"And it is appointed unto men once to die, but after this the judgment." This Scripture is often cited from Heb.9:27, as Biblical support that upon death, we go straight to hell or to heaven. [76] This reasoning is so negligent. Consider if it is said: "It is appointed once to graduate high school, and afterwards go on to college"; in no way does it mean one goes to college immediately upon their graduation. There is no time-factor mentioned here (nor in this Scripture). Yes, you graduate high school first before going to college, but

---

[75] Ps.88:10-12

[76] In Jn.6:39-40, Jesus speaks of raising people up *on the last day.*

there can be any amount of time, even years, before going to college. I don't mean to be insulting, but this sort of reasoning presented by many a Protestant with this Scripture, upsets me! So please, if you will, do give me some slack here in allowing me to vent, for I know not how, with any degree of honesty, to put it otherwise; for to me, the use of Heb.9:27 to substantiate that there is instantaneous judgment upon our death, is a betrayal in the sincere seeking of truth, the whole truth, and nothing but the truth.

Another example of shoddy reasoning is to say that Christ didn't make wine, but grape juice. Are we to believe that at weddings guests were given grape juice to drink? Who then were lauding His "grape juice" and calling it real good wine! For sure, Christ could make the very best grape juice in the whole world, but it would take a lot of prior wine-drinking by these guests to call what then was given to them "good wine". And what of the drink at the last supper, are we to think they drank grape juice after dinner, and not wine? (the footnote here is worth reading in regards to the matter of wine's fermentation).[77]

There are many other findings in his study disclosing

---

[77] In Matt,9:17; Mk.2:22; Lk.5:38; and Lk.5:37 Christ says: *"no man putteth new wine into old bottles; else the new wine will burst the bottles...."* This is due to alcoholic fermentation, as gas is produced, and the pressure will burst a weakened bottle or skin. I quote here a Baptist scholar who wrote to me, in referring to Mt.26:29, where Jesus speaks of the fruit of the vine: "The fruit of the apple tree is apples, not juice;" "the fruit of the orange tree is oranges, not OJ; and the fruit of the vine is grapes, not the juice." (Are we thus to believe they toasted not with wine but with grapes?)

Catholic teachings that he list as invented by man or not Scriptural. I've no doubt, that he did not seek any information from the church in coming to any of his suppositions about the church. He simply was out to get the results he wanted: "The Catholic church is a false church!" That's how his research study began. That's how his "research study" concluded.

I have admiration for this pastor. Though our contact is strained by our contentions, he and his wife always welcome me at the services of their church, treating me with sincerest hospitality at any of their community functions. In his wanting to pastor me, he has shown, that he has a caring heart ... even as I bring forth Scriptural challenges (as Paul wrote, without love, all else is nothing). Let it be known, I had a Mass said for him, and speak out his name softly every time I receive the Eucharist upon my tongue at Mass.

Jesus says the church is the final arbiter of a dispute.[78] Yet a church consisting of a-body-of--true-believers dispersed throughout the many Christian denominations have no accepted authority that can be gone to, to arbitrate a dispute. The Presbyterians would not accept the Baptists decision of a dispute; the Methodists would not accept that of the Catholics; the Evangelicals would not comply with the decree of the Pentecostals; and on and on and on. The body-of-dispersed-true-Christians are thus at a loss in the settling of a dispute in any final kind of a way. Thus this instruction given by Christ to go

---

[78] Matt.18:17

to the church to have a dispute settled, cannot be accomplished.[79] How can that be? It's as if the words of Christ spoken here are spoken in vain. It can't be.

To the contrary, numerous churches are referred to as congregations being in specific locals, and in the Scriptures footnoted below, not a one of them can be inferred as being of a group of dispersed believers.[80]

If you were to be asked: "Where is one to find the truth?" What might be your answer: In the Bible?[81] In your heart? From the pastor of your congregation? From a trusted fellow parishioner? In philosophy? In science?

In his letter to Timothy,[82] Paul wrote that the church *"is the pillar and ground of the truth."*

So: If we go by what Paul wrote, that is to say, if we go by what God has to say in this Scripture ... where should we then seek for the truth? If, indeed, you do agree with God, that the church is where the truth is upheld, and where it's very foundation exist, how then, I ask, can this truth that the church possesses, be acquired by a

---

[79] Mat.18:15-17 Hence Christ would be giving a vain instruction.

[80] Acts15:29, 15:41, 16:5, Rom.16:16, 1Cor.7:17, 11:16, 14:34, 16:1, 16:19, 2Cor.8:1, 8:18, 8:19, 11:8, 11:8, 11:28, 12:13, Gal.1:2, 1:22, 1Thess.2:14, 2Thess.1:4, Rev.3:6-7 (to name but a few).

[81] The teaching of the Gospel only flourished verbally (Tradition), and by letter for centuries. Paintings, stained glass, and statues, were created to reveal the chronicled account of Christ, and the Gospel's message ... helpful to all, especially to the many who could not read. Douay-Rheims Bible precedes the King James.

[82] 1Tim.3:15

congregation of the dispersed-believers, who have no human authority from which to get this truth; instead they are believing that they can be individually taught by the Holy Spirit (but then coming up, as we see, with the predicament of many differing interpretations). So how can this possibly be the means to seeking the truth? It's not reliable (couldn't be more obvious). May my words be honestly spoken: The idea of spiritual self-guidance cannot help but bring about spiritual discord?

Take note: Paul is writing to Timothy (evidently a new elder of the church) with authority. Paul knows if his authority is rejected, there will be confusion and conflict, and this is what he is out to prevent. (can you ever imagine Paul preaching, as some pastors do, that if you disagree with his teachings, to go home and let the Holy Spirit lead you in your own way of interpreting what he had to say?). Let's face it: If everyone can claim their authority comes from the Holy Spirit, then everyone has authority (but this is the same as no one having authority); so differences in doctrine, or of any kind, can't ever be settled with decisiveness.

So instead of our having a Christian doctrine and faith standing in powerful unity for all the world to witness, to be seen as a beacon of the light, a beacon of Truth, we have now multiples of differing and contentious Christian doctrines in the world, with each claiming the Bible is on their side! How can the truth be confused and alienated against itself like this? Christ said to the apostles, *"Peace be unto you"*, [83] advising that His followers be at peace with one another, and not in dissension, rivalry, disagreement, conflict, confusion, contention, dispute, squabbling, clashing, wrangling, misunderstanding, bickering, spats, strife, quarreling, argument, and alienation.

True it is, that the reformation leaders were motivated by valid concerns of corruption within the church's administration (myself: I think it broke Martin Luther's heart to see such corruption going on in the church to which he so gave his all). He could have brought about correction to the church by his dissent ... but instead of taking place as it should have within the church (of which he was a part), he became frustrated by the lack of proper response and rebelled. The results of his rebellion remain with us in our disunity, and an ever, and ever progressing fragmentation; a jigsaw puzzle of opinions and interpretations, which is bringing us chaos within the faith and amongst each other so personally. [84]

Just how are we to possibly know what is true with all these differing beliefs being presented to us? Might it be by the study, study, study of Scripture; or getting an education in theology or history that gains us scholarly degrees of knowledge? Or is it by living a hermit-like

---

[83] Lk.24:36, 1:79; Jn.20:19-21, 20:26; Mk.9:50; Rom.1:7, 14:19; 2Cor.13:11

[84] How personal indeed it gets, as a young couple I know, seemingly so right for one another, have parted due to "doctrinal differences" (even as they each believe in the same Christ as Lord, the same Holy Spirit, and the same Father in heaven).

existence in deep contemplation and prayer? Does it even matter at all what denomination we embrace if we take the sinner's prayer that is in the Protestant's and Baptist's tradition as well as the Catholic's?

One day I was listening to a Baptist pastor speaking in a recorded scriptural debate, say that God did not intend for there to be doctrinal unity. What a shame, I thought to myself, to hear that he thinks this is the truth, and that he must preach this to his parishioners. Is he not mindful that Paul wrote, *"that there be no divisions"?*[85]

While yet a Southern Baptist minister, indeed a budding friend, a Doctor of Theology & Biblical studies, and a former SWAT agent with the FBI (clearly a man of character, who is intelligent, judicious, and surely quite street-smart) who says our denominational differences may be endorsed by God. He goes on to say that, in unity, we all meet as one at the foot of the cross. I see this as just a cop-out means to not confront squarely the dilemma of the multiple divisions so prevalent amongst the Protestant denominations. It is sad to me that he thinks in this way. So much more so, do I believe, must it be to the Father, the Son, and the Holy Spirit, who do live as one, as they view our doctrinal and moral schisms. It is sad, because even those worthy of high esteem and respect, can come to a persuasion of our disparities, that instead of, at least, keeping alive in us an interior hope for the unity that our Lord prays for, give instead a divine sanction to our doctrinal differences and consequent

---

[85] 1Cor.1:10

multiplicity of denominations ... thus contributing to an acceptance of our separations. If even he sought that Christian unity should be in his own denominational belief, there would at least be in his heart a prayerful desire for our oneness.

Luther's reforms have shattered Christianity (this is not at all what he intended). Because many deny a church authority, it cannot be overstated, we have now disheartening divisions in our faith. Had Martin Luther persevered in the needed reforms of the church at that time, *from within the church*, no matter how much time it might have taken, rather than rebelling and conjuring up then his own authority, the church might very well be referring to him today as "Saint Luther." What a blessing he could have been for the faith, instead of now hearing this pastor saying that God did not intend for there to be unity in the faith, and another saying our differences are endorsed by God. So deplorably has the reformation brought with it a predisposition by some to disseminating and fueling doctrinal divisions that exist amongst us, as literally being God's will.

For many a non-believer throughout the world, their witnessing of these divisive convictions in Christianity is more than enough cause for them to judge that there is really no credibility in the message of redemption and salvation in Jesus Christ. Or, in the least, they'll just say they're all good (they're really just passing 'em all off).

Give exceedingly due regard in a most sincere way to this matter ... for the unity of the church is not merely a nice thing; it is an essential attribute in her mission to spread the truth of the Gospel. To repeat: Our unity is significantly beneficial to the propagation of the Christian faith. As a consequence of the divisions amongst us, there exists so grave an impediment to the conversion of the world, and it's openness to the love and the salvation of God that He offers in Christ. In accordance with God's own words, the unity of the faithful is one of the vital issues that will draw people to the truth.[86]

Understandably it will be disputed, even resented by some brothers and sisters of the Christian faith, nonetheless the only candidate for Christian unity is the Catholic Church. Let me step back a moment here, for scrutiny is due of this declaration: Everyone must likely believe that their Christian faith is the truest one. So what merit is there really, to saying that the Catholic Church is the one that is to bring us to unity as the church herself proclaims? Is it not arrogant of the church to proclaim that she is the fulfillment of the Christian faith? On the other hand, if believing it is true, it would be a false humility for the church to politely refrain from saying so. True it is that absolute claims such as this tend to be, by our very nature, provocative to us. Just as it is so in Christ's claim of being the only way to the Father ... He nevertheless presents it as an absolute (which certainly is revolting and ludicrous to those not of the Christian faith). So too, in this manner, does the church claim its fullness of the faith.

As you consider what I write here, I seek not to close the

---

[86] John17:21, 17:23, Eph.4:13, Psalm133:1

door on you to challenge it. Truth is something to be discovered, and when done so, to be voluntarily embraced and surrendered to ... it is never something to be imposed. Thus, I do encourage the sincere examining, scrutinizing, and comparison of the many Christian churches and denominations throughout the world, their faithfulness to the Scriptures, their history, and their effect upon mankind. Here is mine:

In my stating of the Catholic Church's place in the world (and of course, this is not merely a personal opinion of mine), acknowledge, if you will, how she has come to transcend all ethnicities, cultures, and nations, beyond that of all other churches and denominations put together in the spreading of the Gospel. So too, it is a known statistic, that every day she feeds, clothes, shelters and educates more people throughout the world, and in all nations (in some quite underground), than all other organization, both secular and religious, combined.

Declared on-air to be the "citadel of Christianity" by Fox News host, Judge Jeanine Pirro, reveals that the church's proclaiming of the salvation-in-Christ is highly visible and presented to all the world, the secular and religious. The Church has so long a history of speaking out of the salvation in Christ, and the love of God; along with a history of involvement in the world's most serious of affairs. There are as well Catholic churches and shrines at the many sacred places throughout the world: Such as Mt. Sinai, where Moses was given the Ten Commandments; in Rome where Paul was executed by Nero; the tomb of Jesus at Calvary, where He was crucified; the Mount of Olives where Jesus ascended to heaven; and the hill where He gave His notable sermon; to name but so very few. At each of these locations, there exist a Catholic church and/or shrine venerating the site. I venture to say we'll find such at every significant place in Christianity's history. Look as well upon the numerous churches throughout Europe and Asia, some going back a thousand years and much more, and they're Catholic one after the other after the other.[87] Built in stone as they are, this is pretty concrete evidence of the Church's early history and fundamental position in the world's Christian faith.

Avery Dulles, distinguished throughout the world as a great scholar and theologian, wrote (at the time a Presbyterian) of his personal Christian journey:[88]

> The more I examined the more I was impressed with the consistency and the sublimity of Catholic doctrine. Through dark ages and enlightened, through ages of fervor and ages of corruption, under saintly popes and ordinary popes, the treasure of the faith had been preserved intact....Not even the greed and depravity of wicked popes (of whom, be it known, I found but few) had been capable of impairing the integrity of Catholic doctrine. In peril often, the deposit of faith remained

---

[87] One of the oldest being the Pantheon in Rome, built about 126AD, became later a Catholic church in the 7th century.

[88] Avery later became a renowned Catholic Bishop, then a Cardinal (1918-2008).

untarnished and entire...

Surely it was a divine protection which had saved the church through all these centuries from human failings. Like the boat in which Christ slept, the church was tossed by tempests, but was always safe.

The human head of the church, that is the successor to Peter, draws attention and crowds today just as Peter did; for we do read in the Scriptures, how the people tried even to just be in Peter's shadow in their seeking the power of God which they sought from him (as he did explain, it was coming not from him, but from Christ).[89] Yes, some did inappropriately idolize him, just as some have done the popes in all times (which is idolatry and against church teaching and doctrine, but certainly most do not). It is clearly not the man the crowds are drawn to, for before one becomes the head of the church, that is, the Bishop of Rome, he attracts no such attention worldwide honor. It is

---

[89] Acts.5:15 All the popes throughout history have received much attention in the various news media. Even now, 'Time Magazine' named Pope Francis "Man of the Year" (Dec. 2013), and did a dedicated issue on him when he was elected (noting that three million people came to hear him in Rio de Janeiro); there are other publications, too numerous to mention, throughout the entire world, and now even a weekly magazine in Europe, 'Il Mio Papa', has been published exclusively on him ... and, get this, astonishing as it seems, he's even on the cover of the 'Rolling Stone Magazine' (Jan. 2014). Ha! Who'da thought.

his divine office[90] whereby people are drawn to Christ, and give glory to God, by the millions, upon millions, upon millions, throughout all his worldly visits both today and yesterday.

Indeed, as the pope is greeted by the crowds, they do so with extraordinary exuberance and joy (and not just for one particular pope, but for pope, after pope, after pope). How astounding it is that this world-wide attention and attraction of the pope's Christian position in the world's stage has continued for the past two-thousand years, from the poorest of the poor, to the rich and the powerful, and continues to do so even in today's secularized culture and environment.

So too, when the Bishop-of-Rome is being chosen by the church's magisterial assembly of Cardinals, it is major news, covered throughout the free world. Recognized as the head of the Christian community, he is visited by presidents and dignitaries from all nations and all faiths; and when he dies, so too do they attend his funeral service.[91] This is not to mean that popularity denotes

---

[90] John17:4, 22

[91] AP reports say that 4 to 5 million journeyed to Rome to say goodbye to John Paul II at his funeral (April 2005): Never in human history have so many from so many places in the world gathered to pay their final respects. More than a hundred nations were represented. The American President and two former Presidents were present, along with monarchs, prime ministers, and dignitaries, including a large Jewish delegation, and many from Islamic nations. The church is indeed not invisible, it is observed

Godliness ... just pointing out how it is that the world's attention towards Christianity is, by far, foremost upon the Catholic Church like it is upon no other.

Even those who fiend Christianity in a diabolical way, place their focus almost exclusively upon the Catholic church as they enact their evil concoctions and contemptuous anti-Christian rituals in a manner that expresses enmity in some dreadful way (especially upon the sacraments of the church), and particularly they will defile in some hideous, unmentionable manner, the consecrated Eucharist, the body of Christ, or His blood, whenever they can get their hands upon this sacred Host. Satanist will hold, what is referred to as a Black Mass, whereby the Mass is recited in reverse (when knowing of this, Catholics will have a special Mass referred to as a Mass of reparation).

There are terrorist groups extolling a radical Islamic ideology destroying ancient Christian churches, monasteries, and artifacts in Syria, Afghanistan, and Iraq. They are torturing, burning, and beheading by the thousands, anyone not consenting with their creed, all in the name of their god; claiming, as they are, to be waging the final war. Christians are especially being targeted by them throughout the world. One group photo-shopped their black flag atop of the Vatican, and are quoted as saying: "we will conquer Rome". And when they beheaded twenty-one Egyptian Christians, it's reported

---

by all, and is a beacon of light to the entire world (Mt.5:14-16, Lk.11:33).

that they mentioned Rome/Italy as being "the city signed with the blood of the cross." [92]

Pay heed as well to the many involvements that the popes and church elders have had, and do to this day, in all matters affecting our world. Pope John Paul II, it is well attested to, was most instrumental along with President Reagan, in bringing down the Berlin wall. [93] By his visit to Poland, where three million of his fellow countrymen attended the Mass, he inspired so much hope ... bringing empowerment to the Polish people; and being thus of considerable significance in ending their nation's communist rule as he spoke out publicly (a big no-no) against those in power.

In his visit to Ireland in the 70's, over one-million attended the Mass service; another million-plus did so in Boston (1979); three-hundred-thousand in Scotland; In 1979 five million in Mexico, and in 1995 over four million attended in the Philippines; and this is to name but these few of the one-hundred-and-four visits he made throughout the world to country after country after

---

[92] Terrorists in Italy are plotting to attack the Vatican. (God will overcome their evil goals as foretold in Mt.16:18 & Lk.19:43; and as David said in Ps.23:4: *"I will fear no evil"* (easier said than done ... so too, how hard it is to pray, to bless, to love, and to forgive, those who persecute us, as Jesus asks of us to do (Mt.5:44, Lk.6:27, 6:35).

[93] 'NINE DAYS That Changed the World': A video documentary hosted by former U.S. House Speaker Newt Gingrich along with his wife, Calista.

There's a movie, 'Karol, The Pope, The Man', which is of his incredible life and times during the Nazi invasion of Poland, prior to his becoming even a priest.

country ... beckoning people to Christ ... and exalting the dignity of all people and human life.[94]

John Paul II sought to build bridges of dialogue throughout the world with other denominations, even those not of the Christian faith. When visiting Greece in 2001, he met with the head of the Greek Orthodox church who read publicly a list of offences by the Catholic church against the Orthodox church; and the lack of any apology, saying that "There has not been heard a single request for pardon for the maniacal crusaders of the 13th century". It is reported that the pope responded by saying, "For the occasions past and present, when sons and daughters of the Catholic church have sinned by action or omission against their Orthodox brothers and sisters, may the Lord grant us forgiveness". This pope indeed did express that the crusades were a source of "deep regret" for the church.

Just recently, the President of the United States visited Pope Francis to discuss worldly issues of concern (so too have so many of the world's leaders); thus do we see how it is the human head of the Catholic church who especially comes to present the concerns of the world's Christian community to the world's rulers.

Most recently Pope Francis invited the Israeli and Palestinian Presidents to come to the Vatican to pray for peace. Both leaders accepted; and a few weeks later this had taken place, whereby Muslim, Jewish, and Christian leaders prayed together for God to bring peace to their

---

[94] Pope Francis as well has had millions upon millions attend his services and message of Christ's mercy throughout the world.

nations and their people. Just recently too, Pope Francis has been invited by the President to visit; so too by the US Congress to address them; and as well by the U.N. Secretary, to visit and speak in 2015 (a visit that will be of historical measure and sure to get phenomenal attention here and worldwide) ... and these are but the most recent accomplishments and involvements which I can think of, for there have been so many in the two millenniums of the church's history. Even matters not so magnanimous, though of merit, play a role in the church's practices; such as popes presiding over an annual Mass held within the Roman Coliseum where, in its history, Christians and others had once been put to the lions before large cheering audiences.

Let there be due appreciation and sincere praise of the many denominations throughout the world doing countless works of virtue, providing loving care to children, the elderly, the sick, and spreading of the Gospel in their missionary works. But truth be told, no other is advancing the Gospel throughout the world's nations as does the Catholic church, nor providing care and teaching beyond all others combined to those in need. All thanks be to God.

To the Catholic, the church's assemblage of priests and bishops, its magisterium and its pope, are a part of the revelation of Christ in the Gospels. It is religion and institution as developed and authorized by the apostles as we read in the Scriptures. In no way is the church an obstacle placed between God and man as some accuse; she is rather a guider in our faith, a protector, and a truly merciful consoler; and by her long history and prayerful study of the Scriptures for nearly two-thousand years, she is full of spiritual wisdom, and with open arms, she is eager to thoroughly explain the faith in a most thoughtful way, and to describe its history and the mission of the church in the world.

The matter of the church's holiness was addressed to a large public audience, as is customary, in St. Peter's square by Pope Francis (Oct. 2, 2013):

> In the Catholic creed, we confess that the church is 'holy'; we thus affirm the holiness of the church...

> But how can we say that the church is holy, if we see that the church throughout history, during her long journey through the centuries, has experienced many moments of darkness? How can the church be holy if she is made up of human beings, of sinners? Of men who are sinners, women who are sinners, priests who are sinners, nuns who are sinners, bishops who are sinners, cardinals who are sinners, popes who are sinners? Everyone. How can a church like this be holy?

> The church is holy because she comes from God, Who is holy. Who is faithful to her and never abandons her to the power of death and evil. She is holy because Jesus Christ is indissolubly united to her. She is holy because she is guided by the Holy Spirit which purifies,

transforms, and renews [her]. She is not holy by our merits, but because God makes her holy...

Throughout history there has been the temptation to say: the church is just the church of the pure, of those who are entirely coherent, and the rest are to be cast aside. No! It's true! This is heresy. The church is holy, she does not refuse sinners; on the contrary, she welcomes them, she is open even to those who are most distant, she calls to all to allow themselves to be surrounded by the mercy, tenderness, and forgiveness of the Father, Who offers to all the opportunity to encounter Him...

"Do not be afraid of holiness, of letting yourself be loved and purified by God" ... "holiness does not consist in doing extraordinary things, but rather in letting God act. It is the encounter between our weakness and the strength of His grace."

Somewhat in contrast is a Baptist minister, who sang good bass in a singing group, who preached in a very irate tone, how some religions have the body of Christ displayed "With nails through His hands and feet nailed to a cross!" 'How dare they show the Lord in this way!' he indignantly implied. Of course I was bothered that he should be insulting the depiction of the greatest act of love, being God's sacrifice of this Man-on-the-Cross, who voluntarily accepted and allowed His death by torture and crucifixion so as to take away the sins of the world and offer to mankind deliverance from our evils.

While preaching of this kind is not all that typical, that it nevertheless was allowed and came from the pulpit of this Baptist church, shows the bias and thwarted ways some do go to attack and spread their offensive prejudice against the Catholic church and faith; even doing so upon God's act of Love as seen on the crucifix.

Sad it is to know that there are those who in their loathing of the Catholic church, go well beyond calling her a false religion, but rather esteem themselves of having spiritual wisdom in describing the church as "demonic"; "the whore of Babylon"; and the popes being "the anti-Christs"; and that "Catholics are but pagans destined for hell." [95]

---

[95] Denouncing the Catholic Church in this way is a sin. I pray for the Lord's mercy, as He has certainly done and does so for me.

That We

Be

one

✳✳✳✳✳✳✳✳✳

The Matter of No Doubt

"I am saved!"

Jesus brings to our attention a most unsettling of statements; and really I should rather say, even a most frightening of statements: *"Not everyone that saith unto me, 'Lord, Lord', shall enter into the kingdom of heaven, but he that doeth the will of my Father which is in heaven."* Thus is He quoted in Mt.7:21 as He speaks to those professing their faith in Him: In their astonishment, they proclaim, "Lord, have we not prophesied in thy name? and in thy name cast out devils? And in thy name done many wonderful works?" In reply, He'll say to them: *"I never knew you: depart from me, ye that work iniquity."* Good grief ... what a thing to say!

Boy, we can readily see why this will be so great a shock to the depths of their soul to those He so speaks ... for these are people who have professed their faith in Him, and so openly too; those who have been active in their faith; some even having have performed miracles! Imagine that! Likely they brought others to embrace Christ as their Savior. Upon our notice of them, surely we would say, "There goes a real good, upright

Christian." Yet here they are, on their day of judgment, being told that they are not known by Christ! *"depart from me"*, He tells them; He is even accusing them of doing evil!

Doing evil? So too does Paul write in Phil.3:18 (this while they live of course), *"For many walk, of whom I have told you often, and now tell you even weeping, that they are the enemies of the cross of Christ."* Paul is literally crying as he refers to these members of this church as being "enemies of the cross."

Enemies of the cross? But ... but they're avowed members of the Christian church? They're Christians! Did they believe they were saved? Just how can this kind of way of thinking come upon any believer like this? This pronouncement coming upon them from Christ in their judgement (and from the apostle Paul as well while they live), not only is it unexpected, but that which comes from Christ especially seems rather unfair ... doesn't it to you? Understandably, they're indignant about it. Nevertheless, Christ is the Lord, and this is the decree He makes to them at that momentous time.

Who are they? Exist they do among us; for as Christ said, there will be those receiving this most dreadful announcement. Are they Catholics? Or Protestants? Baptists? Presbyterians? Is it me? Is it You? Are they pastors, priest, or bishops; or perhaps individuals secretly, or even openly, living unrighteously as a matter of course in some ways, all the while professing faith in Christ, and perhaps notably attending all the services of their denomination? It sure does seem so incredibly paradoxical for Jesus to say He does not know them, for they lived a life believing and proudly proclaiming they knew Him. Surely all openly professed believers in Christ do not suppose it could ever, ever, ever be them; and all the more so are they quite bona fide in believing so, if they've performed miracles and all (I'll tell yah, if I performed miracles I would certainly believe I was, without question, bound for heaven ... at least I would have before my reading of this Scripture some time ago).

Regarding those given this condemning judgment from Christ, what-oh-what could be so wrong? What could be so, so amiss in someone's faith, and truly seeming to themselves and to others, so genuine a faith, for them to then be deserving of this harsh response from Jesus, whom they call their Lord?

They are even called evil doers! Why so? Is it, as He describes whereby they failed to care for Him, as they did not do so for the least of persons? Is it those, who are like the man unwilling to sell all he has and distribute it to the poor, as Christ asked of him? [96] Has it to do with something of or about Christ, a sacred Truth, which they have denied, perhaps openly denounced throughout their life, and maybe sought even to persuade others to believe as they did and deny as well?

"Are you saved?"

Protestants and Baptists will often ask this question. Most will certainly answer it with a resounding "Yes!"

---

[96] Mt.25:45; Mt.25:34-36; Lk.18:22 (note the worth of works)

Implicit in this outlook is the notion that the human race may be divided into the saved and the unsaved; and the "saved" feeling, at least by some, a cut above those reckoned as "not saved".

What of the judgment after our death that is written of in Scriptures? According to "the saved", they are definitely going to heaven upon their death. But Scripture repeatedly states that there will be a judgment day before Christ. So, of those who assert they are saved, what judgment can Christ make as they have proclaimed that their judgment is already a done deal?[97] (do look into the Scriptures footnoted below).

There certainly are Scriptures that seemingly can be taken as supportive of one's salvation being fixed. Let's examine them if you will: The most cited one being Jn.3:16 *"For God so loved the world, that He gave His only begotten Son, that whosoever believeth in Him should not perish, but have everlasting life";* [98] Another being Rom.10:9 *"That if thou shalt confess with thy mouth the Lord Jesus, and shalt believe in thine heart that God hath raised Him from the dead, thou shalt be saved."* And another Heb.11:1 *"Now faith is the substance of things hoped for, the evidence of things not*

---

[97] Jn.5:24-30, 6:39-40; Mt.10:15; Rom.14:10; 2Cor.5:10; Heb.9:27; 1Thes.4:14-16; 2Pet.2:9, 3:7

[98] Protestants often quote Jn.3:16 as: *"thou shall not perish"*, rather than *"should not perish"* which the KJ reads. This alters its meaning. The Douay-Rheims Bible (which is translated from the Latin Bible and predates the King James) has this passage as: *"may not perish"*, which does, I'd say, have the same consequence as, *should not perish.*

seen." 1John5:13 is another: *"These things have I written unto you that believe on the name of the Son of God; that ye may know that ye have eternal life, and that ye may believe on the name of the Son of God."* Thus, according to their interpretation of Scripture here, salvation is irreversible, and is explained this way in general (and I trust I will describe this justly):

> We can't earn salvation; we are saved by God's grace when we have faith in His Son, Jesus Christ. What is necessary is that you recognize you are a sinner; that Christ died in atonement for your sins; and ask His forgiveness. He knows you and loves you. What matters to Him is the attitude of your heart, your honesty. In accord with Protestant literature and teaching, reciting the following prayer is suggested in accepting Christ as your Savior:'

> *Dear Lord Jesus, I know I am a sinner and in repentance I humbly ask for your forgiveness and that you may come into my heart. I believe you died for my sins and rose from the dead. I now trust and follow you as my personal Lord and Savior.*

In accordance with Catholic teaching, salvation indeed is a gift offered to us by the grace of God. We cannot earn it by any means. But the gift so given can be lost by serious sinfulness or even discarded. So which is true? Fixed, or not? This question is worth sincere scrutiny.

There are, as well, many Scriptures quite supportive of salvation not being fixed, but being rather a lifelong process, and that it can be lost by grievous sin (take note here that God's mercy is infinitely greater than our sins; it can be regained by one's repentance). Let's examine them: A few Scriptures are Phil.1:6 & 2:12, and Mt.10:22: *"Being confident of this very thing, that He which hath begun a good work in you will perform it until the day of Jesus Christ."* (emphasis on *"begun"*); that we *"work out your own salvation with fear and trembling,"* and *"he that endureth to the end shall be saved."* We read in 1Jn.5:16-17 of there being sin which leads to a death, and sin that does not lead to death. 1Jn.5:13 (which was previously quoted as supporting salvation as guaranteed), we read how there is the requirement that we keep God's commandments.[99] So it is that the "believing" in Christ does not stand alone as the means to salvation ... what we do with and after God's gift of salvation matters. As 2Cor.17:10 reads: *"For we must all appear before the judgment seat of Christ; that every one may receive the things done in his body, according to that he hath done, whether it be good or bad."* Solomon puts it this way: *For God shall bring every work into judgment, with every secret thing, whether it be good, or whether it be evil."* [100] Ecclesiastes 12:14, by Solomon, reads: *"For God shall bring every work into judgment, with every secret thing, whether it be good, or whether it be evil."*

Baptists especially will say of someone who sins in a

[99] Deut.8:11
[100] Ecc.12:14

serious way after having repented and confessed Christ as their personal Lord and Savior (believing they were thus saved), that in fact they never were a truly a Christian, nor saved ... for they reason, if you are truly saved, you won't sin seriously. There is inherent in this reasoning that has at its core, though unspoken, an assumption that the truly saved person, the true Christian, will not only not sin seriously, but will *never* sin seriously. In essence, this means that if you claim that your salvation is without-a-doubt fixed, is thus to claim that you know, as well without-a-doubt, that in your entire life's future, you'll never, ever commit serious sin (of course I pray you do not).

Let me repeat this that I may drive this point home to you (and I do so with a sincere heart): If you, in this for-instance, should ever commit serious sin, you had it all wrong from the get-go ... you never were a Christian, and you were never saved; though all along in your life, until that time, you believed you were, and that it was fixed ... and you were being told you were. So it is that even the pastor who is telling you this, is claiming to know that you will never commit serious sin for the rest of your life.

Yes when someone, perhaps in an altar call, or in any way, comes to repent and call upon Christ, they have thus begun their Christian journey of faith given by God's grace. But Jesus doesn't only say to "believe in Him", or to merely confess His name as Lord as if that's all there is to Rom.10:9. There are things required in the "believing-in-Him", as He points out in Mt.7:21 and

Mt.12:50 how we must do the will of His Father.[101]

Here's an explanation on salvation taken both from the Old and the New Testaments, excerpted from a great book by Proffessor Edward Sri, titled: 'Love Unveiled':[102]

> In his first letter to the Corinthians, Paul emphasizes how God saved "all" the Israelites from slavery to Egypt, but "most of them" did not enter the Promised Land (1Cor.10:1-5). He tells how God miraculously parted the waters of the Red Sea so the people could escape from Egypt and how God provided food and drink for them in their journey through the desert. But Paul goes on to stress that God was not pleased with most of them. In fact, many fell into sin and idolatry in the desert and were disinherited. Note how they *all* received the same free gift of being saved from slavery, but *most of them* lost that gift and were not allowed to enter the Promised Land.
>
> Paul then goes on to say that "these things happened to them as a warning" for us. (1Cor.10:11). In other words they were recorded in Scripture "for our instruction". Paul is telling the Corinthian Christians, and all of us, that

---

[101] Ps18:20; Mt.5:12, 5:21-22, 6:1, 7:2, 7:20, 12:36, 16:2, 16:27, 18:23-35; Lk.6:23; Rom.1:32, 2:2-3, 11:22-23; 1Cor.3:8, 10:12; 2Cor.5:10-11(works); 1Thess.5:24; 22:12; Jas2:13, 2:17-18, 5:20; 1Pet.1:7, 1:17, 4:17; 1Jn5:16; Rev.3:2, 3:5, 3:8, 20:12-13, 22:12

[102] Used by permission: Ignatius Press

what happened to the Israelites in the desert could happen to us in our own journey of faith. We must not presume upon the gift of our salvation. Just because we have received Christ's saving grace doesn't mean we automatically will go to heaven. We must be faithful to that gift. Just as many of those Israelites turned away from God and were not allowed to enter the Promised Land, so we Christians will be disinherited from the Promised Land of heaven if we do not remain faithful. Paul warns, "Let anyone who thinks that he stands take heed lest he fall" (1Cor.10:12).[103]

So in summary, there is a distinction between what one might call "getting in" and "staying in". "Getting in" to God's covenant family is a completely free gift. The initial grace of justification – forgiveness of sins and becoming God's sons and daughters – is freely bestowed on us by the Father. There is nothing we can do to earn it. But staying in comes with great responsibility. We must be faithful to the covenant family life. We must never presume our salvation, thinking we could never turn away from this gift. Cooperating with God's grace, we must endeavor to grow and mature as god's children, living ever more in imitation of Christ.

---

[103] For the sake of my Protestant Christian brothers and sisters ... The King James Bible reads: *"Wherefore let him that thinketh he standeth take heed lest he fall."*

This declared salvation is common amongst the Baptists and some Protestants, and is, in my estimation, a grave misinterpretation in their beliefs. Indeed, might such an assumption of guaranteed salvation[104] be quite dangerous as one goes claiming unto God, that in their accepting Jesus into their heart as their personal Lord and Savior,[105] that their salvation is completely accomplished and incontestably assured? Might it be that one may believe all their life that they've understood God's word rightly, fearlessly held Him to His Scriptural "promise" (for God does not lie they point out), and are so gallantly confident of going to heaven; only to discover at their life's end, they didn't?

Look how Peter warns that people may misinterpret the Scriptures ... *even to their own destruction* he says[106] (he must obviously know of some doing so). This is a serious warning coming from Peter, and so very evident it is that there is misinterpretation by some, and that true interpretation is not at all to be taken for granted. Quite to the contrary, according to Peter, it needs to be a matter of utmost concern and scrutiny as to how we may come by such true interpretation.

"And ye shall seek me, and find me, when ye shall search for me with all your heart."[107]

In witnessing about salvation to someone, "Are you 100

---

[104] Ps.19:13
[105] Many revere the very year-month-and-day of doing so.
[106] 2Pet.3:16
[107] Jeremiah 29:13

percent certain you are going to heaven when you die?" is a question that Baptists and Protestants may ask. So magnanimous a question is this! I've never been comfortable with it: To say "No", or even "I don't know", seems as if you are dedicating yourself to hell. It's a gotcha kind of question, for to those who ask, you just gotta say "Yes!" If you do not, you are then confessing a serious lack of faith in God's word, and indeed, you must be going to hell.

But let me turn this question around: "Are you one-hundred percent certain you are not going to hell when you die?" In answering "Yes", are you then construing that Christ has no recourse other than to welcome you into heaven? Evidently so.

Now back to the question posed especially by Baptists: "Are you 100 percent certain you are going to heaven when you die?" I must reply, "No I am not 100 percent certain I'm going to heaven when I die."

I cannot ever imagine being before the Lord upon my judgment, and declaring to Him, "Lord, I am saved." For me, at that moment, even in sincerest reverence, I'll surely not be saying ...

"I have repented and confessed You as my personal Lord and Savior, and I am saved."

or

"By the shedding of Your blood I am saved."

(or any such thing)

105

True it is that these Scriptures reveal the ways and means by which Christ won and offers us salvation, and greatest of thanks is due Him for doing so. But to make claim upon our death that salvation is assured, I think is a flaunting way to present one's self to Christ. Rather than being humble in one's faith, and at His mercy, one is instead boldly claiming to Him that their Scriptural interpretations are theirs to make, and thus placing aside, I might even say pushing aside, any notion of a judgement that is to come upon them as Christ so deems.[108] As 2Cor.17:10 reads: *"For we must all appear before the judgment seat of Christ; that every one may receive the things done in his body, according to that he hath done, whether it be good or bad."*

To be presenting one's self to Christ in this self-assured and self-convinced manner, there is, so it seems, no fear of the Lord. No fear of God? How divergent this is to David's Psalm111:10, *"The fear of the Lord is the beginning of wisdom."* Solomon puts it this way: *"Fear God, and keep his commandments: for this is the whole duty of man ... For God shall bring every work into judgment, with every secret thing, whether it be good, or whether it be evil."*[109]

So to ask you: Do you, who believe you are saved, think it's right to stand before the Lord upon your passing, and say to Him, that according to God's word, your salvation is promised to you, and that since God is not a liar, you

---

[108] Proverb 9:10, Psalm 111:10
[109] Ecc 12:13-14

are saved? (this comes across to me, and I say this with compassion, not as having faith in Christ by humbly surrendering yourself in trust to His mercy and in trust to His judgement, but rather as being adamant and insistent with the Lord that you are saved).

"For we are saved by hope", reads Romans8:24, as it goes on to say, *"but hope that is seen is not hope: for what a man seeth, why doth he yet hope for?"* Yet of those who claim their salvation is guaranteed and fixed, they need not "hope" as the Scriptures describe, for they have faith-in-their-faith, thus believing they may, and indeed that they should, boldly and confidently proclaim: "I am saved!"[110] Not to proclaim their salvation as assured would be lacking in the quality of their faith in the promised word of God, as they so deem it ... for doubt, in their understanding, is not to stand strong in the Lord.

In no regard do they see such a self-assured declaration as a lacking in humility before Christ.

All I can envision myself saying while my heart (so to speak) may well be pounding, and my soul trembling, in fear of being before such Goodness, is:

"Lord, in your goodness, please have mercy on me."

Sinner that I am (though indeed I want not to sin), how I hope I do say this with true conviction and a contrite heart, for I've no doubt the only way that I may be saved, is by the granting of His mercy. Such is my hope.

---

[110] Rom.8:24, 12:12, 15:4, 15:13, 1Cor.9:10, Acts23:6,

After all is said and done, as mentioned before, it comes down to "Who do you trust?" You may trust your pastor, and thus bring to him your questions on salvation. In recognizing that this is a serious matter, you do so sincerely to seek the truth about from him.

First off he may likely quote the Biblical verses, Jn.5:13, Jn.6:47, and Rom.816 which he believes in his heart do express God's promise of salvation.[111] They read: *"These things have I written unto you that believe on the name of the Son God: that ye may know that ye have eternal life, and that ye may believe on the name of the Son of God."* ... *"Verily, verily, I say unto you, he that believeth on me hath everlasting life."* ... *"The Spirit himself beareth witness with our spirit, that we are the children of God."* Thus will he say to you that this is Biblical proof of a fixed salvation. It is God's promise.

He may present his further reasoning of Biblical truth:[112]

> When you receive Jesus Christ as your Lord and Saviour, you enter into a relationship with God. You become a child of God (Jn.1:12). You are born into a family (Jn.3:3-7). The Bible compares this spiritual birth into God's family with the physical birth into your earthly family. When you were born as the child of your father and mother, a relationship was established. Even though you may disown your parents, or

---

[111] 1Jn.3:15, Acts16:31, Rom.8:1, Jn.3:16, Eph.1:13-14, Jn.10:28-30, Heb.6:18-20, Eph.1:6

[112] Taken from: Ministry127.com

they disown you, you cannot change the relationship—they are still your parents and you are still their child...

Some would argue and say our relationship with God is broken when we sin and we cease to be His child. This is simply not true. Our fellowship with God is broken, but not our relationship. When David had committed adultery and murder, he prayed in confession to God, *"Restore unto me the joy of thy salvation"* (Psalm51:12). He did not pray, "Restore unto me thy salvation." He did not need to, David's relationship with God had not been altered, just his fellowship and joy.

The reasoning presented by this pastor is not irrational.[113] But is it true? Let's presume this is your Protestant or Baptist pastor: How do you know if what he says here to you is true to God's word? For instance, he makes a distinction of David's praying "Restore unto me the joy of thy salvation," contrasting it to his not praying "Restore unto me thy salvation" as being verification that David's salvation was not lost by his sins, only his joy was lost. Or whereby he says some will argue that we lose our child-relationship with God by committing sin, as he points out that we lose only our fellowship with God (certainly the Catholic church would not claim we lose our child-relationship with God no matter what we do).

---

[113] Fair to say, I trust, neither is the reasoning presented in this book.

You might ask yourself by what authority does he proclaim that his understandings of these Scriptures and others are correct, and thus that he speaks the Truth? Perhaps you seek an answer to this by knowing of the history of the denomination which he is in; or in knowing of his own extensive study of theology; maybe it's in knowing of his deep prayerfulness, or knowing of his exemplary way of life, that leads you to believe what he says.

But alas ... there's another pastor, at another church ... he speaks differently on the matter of salvation. He too quotes the Bible, and he too presents a reasoning that is rational. Why not trust what he has to say? There are many that do. He too may have extensive study in theology, maybe he has a doctoral degree in Biblical history; maybe he speaks powerfully and forceful and is convincing in this manner; or perhaps simply speaks well and gives a sermon with much elaboration; he too is very prayerful, and leads an exemplary life. Those that attend his church think yours is in error; and those attending yours think they're wrong.

How do you choose one over the other as presenting the Truth? And as you do make your choice, why do you make that choice? Do you make your choice by looking upon the attributes mentioned of the pastors? Or do you look upon your own Biblical knowledge; your own prayerfulness; or your own moral goodness? Or might you rather choose the one that agrees with your own views on the matter of salvation?

The Baptist pastor says in his blog, "God does not want you to live in a fog. He wants you to know that you are His child." Yet here you are, God's child, having to make this choice of whose truth to believe.

And so it is, as each and every denomination, makes claim to their own Scriptural interpretations as the Truth (claiming it's the "authoritative word of God"); yet indeed you are left in a fog, and left there on your own ... for where there is for you no wholly trusted single human authority of the Truth of Christ's revelations, there is no hope of ever being out of the fog.[114]

The Catholic Church, while prudently questioned by many as it should be, presents very credible claim that it was begun by Christ,[115] and that His Church will not cease, that His Church cannot cease ... as indeed Christ, by His authority, so bestowed upon the apostle Peter in saying to him, *"And I say also unto thee, That thou art Peter, and upon this rock I will build my church; and the gates of hell shall not prevail against it."* It's as clear as day, surely to me, that Peter was given the reigns to the Church which Christ ordained for him to be its on-earth human head. Jesus even goes on to grant to Peter

---

[114] It is prudent to consider who that single human authority may be ... but there needs to be one (so ordained by Christ) ... if not, truth for us will be obscured by the fog of multiple interpretations.

[115] See references for further study in this regard. Because of the heresies that had developed the Christian church came to be called Catholic/universal to distinguish it from them, and thus, to insure the integrity of the Gospel. Even the existence of ancient churches being Catholic can be seen standing still throughout Italy and all of Europe.

incredible authority, as He says to him, *"And I will give unto thee the keys of the kingdom of heaven: and whatsoever thou shalt bind on earth shall be bound in heaven: and whatsoever thou shalt loose on earth shall be loosed in heaven."* Thus has Jesus placed in Peter's hands astounding trust.[116] Thus did the Church begin, ordained upon a man as its leader along with the other eleven apostles, that the message of God's salvation was to be spread throughout all nations to the end of time.

As a Catholic, we trust Christ by trusting in His Church, mandated by Him to spread the Gospel throughout all nations ... a Church which must, I repeat, which must, exist to this day for Christ said it would. A Church whose elders, both in its beginning and throughout its history, would obviously know better than to ever, ever allow it to cease in its existence by such a negligent and irresponsible an oversight in the ordaining of successors to themselves. To think they did not do so is a reasoning that I find without merit.

To repeat:

"For we are saved by hope, but hope that is seen is not hope: for what a man seeth, why doth he yet hope for?" [117]

The hope of salvation is a hope that can inspire us to willingly and unreservedly surrender our self before God with true humility; it is a hope that is based on the belief that our salvation is made possible by the sacrifice and

---

[116] Doing so even of the man who betrayed Him.

[117] Rom.8:24, 12:12, 15:4, 15:13, 1Cor.9:10, Acts23:6

victory of Christ on the cross; it is a hope that by our repentance, our heavenly life is a most real possibility (thank you God for this hope). No greater a hope can be had for mankind! This hope is a gift offered by the grace of our Creator in His love for mankind.

It takes faith in Christ to hope in Christ. It takes trust in Christ to hope in Christ. It takes trust in His judgement to hope in Christ.

So it is that our Catholic hope upholds its trust and faith in Christ by refusing to take our salvation, presented as it is in the Scriptures, as assured, believing this call in finality, is His to make, and only His to make ... for He is the Judge, He is the Savior, and He is the Lord.

That We
Be
one

✳✳***

The Matter of Blessed Mary

Mary was the first person to so lovingly touch Jesus; to hold Him; to kiss Him and greet Him. As the first person to say 'yes' to God's plan of salvation ... she is the first Christian.

Now many do believe the Catholic Church is worshipping the mother of Christ. They are sincere about this, and their concerns are valid if there be any worship of her, for it would indeed be idolatry. The Church teaches against all forms of idolatry.

I am myself just beginning to have an understanding of her. As I've thought about it more and more, she sure is special! In the reading of her Magnificat (Luke1:37-49), I've come to grasp for one thing, that it is her very flesh, it is her very blood, which God chose to use, to infuse, in the forming of His Son as a human person. "Wow!" Our Father literally put her very blood and flesh into the human Body of His Son. Our Father entrusted Mary with the fetus of His Son in her womb ... for her to nourish and to care for at this stage of His development; and upon His birth, with her loving touches, her voice, her eyes, and her milk. She certainly is "in Christ", in a way like no other person on earth. There's no worship in saying any of this ... its but a matter of the truth of those circumstances.

"Whatever He sayeth unto you, do it" So told Mary to the wedding guests ... being thus, the first written words of her telling people to follow whatever her Son says to do. So too did she act as an advocate for them to Christ when she spoke to Him about there being no more wine at the wedding. He evidently was persuaded by her.

Now to ask: Just what did Mary mean, indeed what did God mean, by saying that all generations shall call her blessed?[118] After all, Christ speaks of many blessed people in His sermon on the mount ... so why did God make it a point for us to know that she, that she herself, says this ... of her-self? And that it would be so, as she says, for all generations.

God also let us know that Elisabeth didn't just say to Mary that she was blessed, but that she did so in a loud voice[119] *"Blessed art thou among women!!!"* Did she shout because Mary was a distance away? Or does God want us to know that Elisabeth, and her child who jumped in the womb, had experienced the presence of Mary's blessedness so profoundly, that Elisabeth just blurted out the strong heartfelt sense she had gotten of it? So ... how about you? Do you call her blessed? The Word of God says we should. Doesn't it?

---

[118] Lk.1:48
[119] Lk.1:42

Some rather point out that Mary is blessed *among* women (emphasis on "among"), as if to mean that she is blessed just as other good women may be ... no more, no less. Are we really to think that she does not rise above and beyond all other women (and men) who have ever existed and will yet come?

I asked a Baptist Pastor I know, "Do you think, that when Jesus refers to His mother as "woman" in John2:4, God is showing us that Jesus sees her just as He does any other woman?" His one-word reply to this question, and I quote, was, "Yes." So ... this pastor, who surely loved his mother in a special way, certainly not seeing her as just "any other woman", places his love for his mother as being superior to the love of Jesus for His mother. Imagine that.

How would you feel if someone said of you that you see your mother as just "any other woman"? How does Jesus feel about such a thing being said of His mother? Offended? You think?

How to explain why He referred to her as *"woman"*, I really don't know: Of one thing I am sure ... in no way did He see His Mom as just any other woman. Indeed to do so would be for Christ to break the commandment of God to honor thy mother ... and as "any other woman", it would certainly be failing to do that.

Here's something I've personally reflected upon: When the apostle's full grasp of Christ as the Lord and Savior of the world really, really, hit home, you know, of His divinity; of their hearing God's voice from heaven saying,

117

"This is my beloved Son"; of witnessing His death and then rising back to life; of His ascension into heaven before their very eyes ... after all this and so much more ... how would they then have viewed Mary who remained with them? It goes without saying that they would love her dearly; but so too, they must have seen her as so extraordinarily and special a person ... they just had to be in awe of her, for she gave birth to this man whom they are now utterly convinced is divine, is God's Son, and is indeed, Himself God. How could they not be astonished and in phenomenal wonderment of her? Supposin' they had then photography, can there be any doubt that some might likely have photos of her on their walls? You think Christ in seeing this when He had returned to them, would have raised His objection, saying how they are distracting their attention towards Him, and even worshipping her? Or might He be pleased to see His mother's photo (or a whittled statue) displayed in affection of her? How about you? Do you get bothered in any way to see your son or daughter having a photo of your mom on their wall?

You see the point I'm making here? She's the mother of this divine person, their Lord, the Son of God. Surely they would have asked her to pray for them; considering that her prayers just might, you know, get special attention from Jesus? [120] There is no worship here of

[120] The term 'prayer' has two meanings: One is a form of worship; the other is merely "to request" (as in saying to someone, "pray tell..."). 'Praying to Mary' is just that - asking of her to pray for us, to be an advocate; just as we ask others to do. She is alive, as surely you know; she lives in heaven; and just as she did on earth, she must have the loving attention of her Son. We

Mary by them, nor now by us, just the reasoning of a reality that surely did exist amongst the apostles and others at that time (I'll bet too that she had many stories to share with them about Jesus that only a mother would know).

Consider that when on the cross, Jesus entrusted His mother to an apostle (whom we believe is John). He told him, *"behold thy mother"*. Now wait a minute! She's not his mother! If she had other sons, why did Christ not entrust her to the eldest?[121] Not to do so would be an insult to him and all the family ... and a most serious defiance of Jewish custom and law.[122]

What Jesus did here certainly conveys the concern He has for His mother. So I ask, why did God want for us to know that Jesus did this? It must be quite significant, for Christ says this to him while in great agony on the cross and in the throes of death. In essence, it seems reasonable that Jesus told the apostle to accept Mary as his mother in a spiritual kind of way. And when this apostle told the others of what Jesus said, what did they make of it? Surely to *"behold thy mother"*, as Christ had

---

believe, as Paul wrote in Romans 8:38, that nothing separates us from the love of God ... and that there is only one-body-of-Christ (here and in heaven).

[121] The claim that Mary had other sons, is not supportable by Scripture. In the Hebrew/Aramaic language, there were no words for cousin, nephew, etc. Blood relations such as these were referred to as brothers and sisters (note Gen.14:12-16 whereby Lot is referred to as the brother of Abram, though, in fact, he is his nephew)

[122] Jewish custom unconditionally decreed that a widower be entrusted to her son as first choice and no one else.

said to him, and *"behold thy son"* to His mother, must have had profound, and even mysterious implications to them. Though their reactions are not written of, this statement by Christ to the apostle must have given them reason to deeply ponder: "What about Mary, and who is she to us?" ... surely this statement of Christ's warrants the same sincerest ponderings of ourselves.

What an agony of agonies it must have been for Mary to witness the pain of her Son, her child, and to hear Him scream as He was being tortured (with no one by His side to console Him, or even to just say, "I love you"); to hear Him speak of His thirst when on the cross; to witness His slow, horrendous death before her very eyes, so powerless to stop it, or to help her Son in any way.

During her insufferable grief, might she have pondered the words of the Rabbi, when the infant Jesus was dedicated at the temple? *"Yea, a sword shall pierce through thy own soul also, that the thoughts of many hearts may be revealed."* [123] This is undoubtedly a timeless statement, and a most profound one, so indeed do I ask ever so solemnly: "Just what has Mary to do with the thoughts of many hearts?" Whose hearts? Whose thoughts? And to whom are they revealed? She's but a human, yet, to put it in different words, God says by virtue of her heart's being pierced with deep pain, the hearts of others will be revealed. Indeed, as this is coming from God, this Scriptural revelation is eternal and significant, and brings to light her perpetual

---

[123] Luke 2:35

involvement in and upon the Christian faith and faithful.

Certainly most Christians see Mary as of great importance in God's plan of salvation: For it is by her cooperation with God, whereby Christ's sacrifice and redemption entered into the earthly domain. Now of course, God could have chosen another woman. But He chose her. God made a particular choice of her; His choice was a perfect choice. To think, as some do, that God's choice of her was that of just any woman is belittling and insulting of God's judgment and choice. Yes, she is special indeed, for it is literally through Mary, that the Savior came into the world as man: And when Jesus bled on that cross, it is also her blood that poured out (for it is her blood and her flesh which God had literally infused into His Son's incarnate body and blood).

Because she is the mother of Jesus Christ, Catholics (and others) refer to her as the mother of God, to which there is objection by many Protestants and Baptist. This is understandably so, if this was to mean she existed prior to Christ or to God the Father. Of course it does not mean this! But ... to not refer to her as the mother of God, would imply a reluctance about the Divinity of Jesus. Simply put: Jesus is Divine. He and God are one. Mary is His mother.

We read of the prophesy by Isaiah (7:14), that the Lord will give a sign of the coming of the Messiah ... *"Behold, a virgin shall conceive and bear a son, and shall call His name Immanuel.*" So it is, that Mary is that sign. Along with her place in Christianity, it is as well in this manner of recognition, that she is represented in paintings and statues. A sign ... *the sign* ... of His promise (suppose the sign had instead been a tree, there would be images and icons of that tree presented in the churches to show to us God's sign in history of the coming of the Lord).

Thus it is, were there no other reason, she would receive acclaim by the Catholic Church. This is not worship any more than it is to be looking upon the icon of the cross inspiring one to an awareness of the victory of Christ over death, or a crucifix presenting to us the extent of God's love and sacrifice for mankind. The icons of the cross or the crucifix are no more to be worshiped than is an icon of Mary (while each serve a purpose in pointing us to Christ).

Further regards of her place and importance in God's plan of salvation can be observed even into the future, as we read of the woman overcoming Satan in Rev.12:1-8. Some want to believe the woman here is symbolizing the church. Sure doesn't come across that way to me at all ... nor so to His Church.

"My soul doth magnify the Lord",[124] said Mary. Now that's a phenomenal statement for anyone to make! Why in heaven's name, would she say *"her soul magnifies the Lord?"* To put it mildly, it's a pretty brash statement for her to make. Think about it ... how can any human

---

[124]   Luke1:46

person dare to think their soul could magnify the Lord? To not put it mildly: It's ludicrous! It's preposterous! It's outrageous![125] So why would she say such a thing as this?

Moreover what does this mean for us? (a point to ponder here as well, is that a soul lives forever). Could it possibly be that God is telling us that the mother of Jesus brings a sort of focus upon the Lord? An undying focus? An eternal magnification? Rather sounds like it ... wouldn't you say? But how can a human person do this forever?

The angel, in greeting Mary, didn't use her name at all. He addressed her as, *"Hail full of grace ... "*[126] Now what does it mean for her, or anyone for that matter, to be "full" of grace (and would an angel use this rather formal way of addressing her in an unintended manner)? Now if it is so that Mary is truly "full" of grace, completely full, can she as well have sin within her? So too to ask as well, would the Father want for His Son to be bathed and infused by flesh and blood that is tainted, even ever, ever, ever so slightly, with sin? (just askin' you know). Thus might we give due and deepest of reflection and thought as to her nature in this regard?[127]

---

[125] Unless, of course, that it's truly so.

[126] Lk1:28 The Douay-Rheims Bible used for centuries and pre-dating KJ, has "Hail full of grace". But the KJ translators decided their translation was better and have this verse as: "Hail, thou that art highly favored".

[127] What of Romans3:23 which states that "All have sinned ...?" Reading the verses here in context (3:1-23) shows that the author is speaking of the Jews and their most sinful ways (certainly Mary would be excluded from his comments in verses 11-18).

In doing so, consider how the ancient Jews went through such great and so costly an effort to use the purest of gold in building the Ark of the Covenant (for within this vessel was to be the stone tablets of the Ten Commandments being, of course, sacred to them). As all things are possible with God, is it so out of place to believe, or at least to consider the belief, that the Father would want and have His Son to dwell in a pure vessel, a holy womb, completely free of the stain of sin? Surely this would be most fitting for the Son (if, that is of course, it's possible for God to do this).

Now you may ask, didn't Mary need salvation? It's a good question. Indeed this matter was seriously considered and grappled with by the elders in the early time of Christianity ... and yes, she did. She, as we all are, is completely dependent on God's saving grace. The key difference upheld by the Church is that Mary received, by the grace of God, her salvation at the moment of her conception ... as the Father prepared for His Son a holy vessel, an entirely holy flesh, an entirely holy blood, an entirely holy person, entirely full of grace. John Paul II once said, "Mary was redeemed in an even more wonderful way, not by being freed from sin, but by being preserved from sin."

* * *

Now to consider a most serious accusation believed by many that the Catholic church engages in idolatry of Mary: This is a serious charge and deserving of a thorough response. I will quote here comments made by Catherine Rose (Catholic blogger and wife of author

Devin Rose referenced herein):[128]

> I understand how someone who is not Catholic
> would think "Idol worship alert!" when they see
> a Catholic making an act of affection to a statue
> of a human person.

Take note that some, be they Catholics and non-Catholics alike, will kneel in prayer before a cross, a crucifix, or a Bible. Of course if someone were to say to the Protestant that kneeling and praying in front of a cross was the equivalent to worshipping and treating the cross as an idol, they would say that they weren't praying to the cross, but to the one-true-God whose Son was nailed to the cross (amen to that).

In the aforementioned blog, Rose goes on to compare how in a football game, for instance, a player who has made a great run might be carried high by the team's members to honor his achievement; or how a man may be down on one knee in proposing marriage to a woman; so too how we have statues and other works of art of those who have accomplished great things in human history (such as Noah, Abraham, Moses, David, President Lincoln, Martin Luther King, Gandhi, and so many others). The carrying of a statue, perhaps of David in a procession honoring him, is not worship of David, and is no different than the carrying of the football player in his honor, or of a statue of mother Mary in her honor.

---

[128] devinrose.heroicvirtuecreations.com/blog (used by permission).

Catholics believe that we can have relationships with Christians who have already gone ahead to heaven [for the body-of-Christ is one-body here on earth and in heaven].[129] I understand the discomfort that a non-Catholic must feel, she says, when they see affection shown toward a statue of a saint...It is similar to kissing the photo of a husband who has been gone too long in Iraq, or caressing with affection a special blanket sewn by a grandmother who has died. These objects help fill the void that exists when we cannot physically be with those we love. We are not worshiping the statue [or the blanket], but merely showing affection for the person whose memory the statue [or blanket] evokes.

With all of the above said, she adds, I think it is important to recognize that idolatry of saints is possible, just as idolatry of any created thing is possible. I can idolize my free time, my money, my physical health; I can idolize my husband or my children.

In accord with the Catholic church and faith, to idolize a saint, or anyone, or anything, is doing so in spite of the contrary teachings of the church.

Just as the mother of Jesus surely did in spirit for the apostles and others (especially when Christ had departed

---

[129] Romans8:31-39

from earth), she brings us closer to Christ as her soul lives on and continues to bring focus to Jesus throughout time. And do take note that all that is mentioned in her regard, is not for her sake, but for the sake of the Son of God. This is a pertinent point not to be overlooked.

Hence, this is what God presents to us so very distinctly in the Scriptures, that of Mary's most extraordinary nature and, of course, He does not worship her ... thus we too, who recognize and do openly embrace this remarkable exceptionalism and her eternally active place in our Christian life as God has pronounced, are thus responding in truth to what God reveals to us of Mary, and what He wants of us.

Nothing more ... and ... nothing less.

* * *

Nevertheless in regards to Mary's magnanimous and so glorious a place in God's redemption for mankind, there is no salvation in the blessed mother of our Lord .... Salvation is only in Christ.

That We

Be

one

The Matter of Faith

Our Christian faith is a mystery.[130] Yet, only faith can ultimately provide a clarification that is sufficient, as reason falls short of doing so, though it is helpful.

Christ said that with faith we can move mountains. Surely that mountain may well be ourselves. Still indeed, our heart's yearning for truth, that silent pull of the Holy Spirit, brings many to sincerely seekthe truth, the whole truth, and nothing but the truth ... and to grasp it in the Christian faith (this book is written especially to those who have this faith in Christ).

How might faith be described? I quote Thomas Aquinas (a most prominent saint to Catholics):

> I adore you O hidden God
> When I contemplate you,
> My mind and heart
> Fail to grasp you.

That's faith.

---

[130] 1Tim.3:9

There's much to be said of his faith, for even when God is silent, he believes in Him and seeks Him in prayer. He needs no miracles; he need make no frivolous claims of apparitions (as some do, apparently needing such to be convinced of God's existence and involvement).[131] Rather he believes that it is his mind and his heart that fall short of grasping the always-present God.

Now without faith in the instructions of Christ to Peter, that He would start His church upon him; and the promise of Christ to Peter that this church would never, ever, fail ... then the continued existence of this church goes un-recognized, refuted, and by some, condemned.

Without faith in the words of Christ to Peter, that what he binds or loosens on earth, is so done in heaven ... then Peter's having of such divinely-given authority and trust, likewise is un-recognized, refuted, and by some, condemned.

Without faith, in the instructions of Christ to the apostles, then their Godly ordained gifts, which includes the forgiveness of sins, are spoken of as the height of arrogance rather than as the height of faith.

Without faith in the testaments and commandments of Christ, a faith that goes well beyond our human understanding, then the belief in His body and His blood being truly present in the Holy Communion is seen as "hocus-pocus".

Note that throughout the Scriptures, never does Christ,

---

[131] Emphasis here is on those claimed in a frivolous manner.

nor anyone, ever refer to His instructions in regards to His body and blood as symbolism or just representing His body and blood; yet I hear so often coming from a non-Catholic pastor in their sermons that it "represents" or is "symbolic" of His body and blood (where do they get this from?). Some will emphasize that it's *in remembrance* (as if somehow this invalidates that Christ says, *"It is"* His body; and *"it is"* His blood). Are not His spoken words here enough reason to believe this?

So far from symbolic are His words here, for we see that Christ makes it a point to highly exalt His commentary as He refers to them as *"the new testament"*. A *"new testament"* surely doesn't seem to be something symbolic. And being His "new testament", can we infer that this is a commandment that, if we love Him, we are to accept?[132]

Indeed, the Scriptures do mention that Jesus's remarks here were unacceptable for many of those present: They remain so for many present in this time.

Yet, might we yield that what our senses fail to fathom, may be grasped through our faith's consent?

---

[132] Mt.26:28; Mk.14:24; Lk.22:20; 2Cor.3:6; Heb.9:15(again to mention: equates "testament" with "covenant"); Jn.14:15, 14:21, 15:10; Mt.15:9; Mk.7:7

That We
Be
one

✳✳✳✳✳✳✳✳✳

The Matter of Trust

As stated in 2Tim.3:16, it is profitable to use Scripture in support of a belief or doctrine. In due course though, the Christian accepts or rejects a Scriptural teaching based on how he or she answers the innermost question: "Who do I trust?"

So ... why do we, why do I, why do you, trust who you trust?

In referring to the many denominations, I asked the Baptist Pastor I know, "Who am I to trust?" he replied in writing: "Trust none of them!" "And do not trust me!" "I am not without fault and errors." "Stick to Scripture", he stressed: "God has spoken the final Word!" "Trust God and His Son only." He quoted Proverbs3:56 *"Trust in the Lord with all thine heart and lean not on thine own understanding. In all thy ways acknowledge Him. And He shall direct thy paths."* "God, is speaking from and through the Scriptures." He writes: "Let Him interpret to us by the Holy Spirit in us." [133]

So, as I understand him here, when reading the Scriptures, that by the Holy Spirit within us, we will be

---

[133] His underlining, and all quotes are verbatim.

directed to the Truth for God will interpret what we read by virtue of our sincere asking. All the same, he says I'm not to trust him ... though he, by inference, is surely "sticking to Scripture" ... thus, by the Holy Spirit, God must be directing him. God is then, as he says, consequently doing the interpreting to him. Hmmm? Now I ask, if God is interpreting for him, as he says of someone who is sticking to the Scriptures, then why can't I trust him? How can he be in error, as he says he can be, if the interpreting of Scripture is being done for him by God? Does this make sense to you?

What a heartbreaking consequence there is to this autonomous way in the seeking of Scriptural discernment; for in consequence, there are numerous Christian denominations throughout the world (and in every town) ... as each pastor, each parishioner, in seeking Truth in this individualistic manner, indeed are leaning on their own understanding. According to the Protestants and Baptists, as a Catholic I am in error in many of my beliefs (though I ask for guidance from the Holy Spirit) ... then why can't they be in error as they ask for the same guidance? Besides, why should I trust the Baptist Pastor who says my Catholic faith and doctrines are wrong, when he says I should not trust him?

So who can we trust? Is there no one at all?

What we now have is that each denomination is believing and adamantly proclaiming that they have the authoritative word of God: As this person or this pastor has one Holy Illumination of Scripture; while another pastor's Holy Spirit has for him a conflicting one which he preaches; and some yet another; and them another; and those around the corner yet another; and still another; and another; and another ... and on it goes. This is wild, nonsensical, zany, farcical, irrational, ridiculous, and unreasonable!

Of course they differ! Just in looking upon the Baptist denominations: we have a First Baptist church; a Second Baptist church (which may or may not differ with the first); certainly differing from them both, are the Southern Baptists; and then there are those who, in their very name, voice their autonomy, they being the 'Independent Baptists'.

I'm not meaning here to pick on the Baptists; they strive better than many to be morally good and spiritually minded people; and certainly we share Christ in common in our faith. It's just that there is something wrong with this picture, and to make matters worse, the Christian community in general, has become complacent of our having these multiple beliefs, and thus is nonchalantly accepting of this serious faulty state of affairs. Let it be said: God is not the author of this confusion. And to repeat, as G.K. Chesterton put it: "We do not really need a religion that is right where we are right. What we need is a religion that is right where we are wrong."

You know who's gratified with our divisions and multiple beliefs? The Master of Deception.

Having been myself of the Protestant faith for a time, and even of no faith, I certainly want not to be imposing and certainly not condemning. I do want to show respect; and I chose to make use of the King James Bible here that I may speak the Protestant and Baptist beliefs in a manner which for them is acknowledged and comfortable. I know too I've criticized at times (and I have thought of softening my words), but I really want to be up-front in my dialogue ... though as I do so challenge, I do want to be of love in my findings of fault as best I can, even as I write in a way that is at times blunt.   And let me say, who can quote the most Scripture, be the best debater, write a letter, write a book, or know more Biblical history, is not the winner here. This is not a contest. It's a quest and dialogue for truth, and an appeal from my heart to yours, of Christianity's need to be one.

That we be one, as Christ prays, is a timeless prayer. Let us appreciate the common and mutual grounds of our faith. Of course, in addressing the differences in our faith, we need to respect one another even in our disagreements (some of which are serious). Still, though the word is overused, and even mis-used, let the truth be told, and celebrated, that we are to love one another. We need to love one another with gentleness and patience, with kindness, tolerance, and forgiveness. This ain't always so for us in our human nature ... still it is what God ask of us. God is Love. Love seeks harmony and union. Love seeks truth and loves truth. Love seeks trust and begets trust

In many areas of our lives we trust others who know

more than we do. We trust the doctors who prescribe our medicines; the surgeons who cut us open; we trust the engineers who design our buildings and bridges; the pilots who fly our planes; and the dentists who pull our teeth. Are we to be without anyone here on earth, in the most crucial of all of life's matters, who are trustworthy and knowledgeable where the revelations of Christs are concerned?

To *believe in* Jesus and His salvation ... there needs to be trust not only in who Jesus is, and the means of salvation He accomplished for us, but as well we must believe in His testimony; His instructions; and His commands.

To *believe in* Jesus, is to be like Peter (imperfect as he was), who in Jn.6:67-68, when others were finding it so, so hard to accept what Jesus was saying of the bread and wine being His body and His blood, replied to Christ; *"Lord to whom shall we go? Thou hast the words of eternal life."*

That's trust.

Peter may not have completely understood just what Jesus meant, but even still there was no wrangling at all by him. He didn't cross-examine, he didn't bicker, he didn't quibble in the least with what Christ was telling him; and he didn't go looking for Scriptures in the Old Testament Bible to reason out otherwise what Christ may have meant as if it were different from what He spoke. He makes no attempt to disparage what Christ was proclaiming. Peter believes in Christ. His belief has him accepting of the words of Christ plain and simple: For to this disciple, to do otherwise didn't even come to his mind.

Just think, would a loving Father leave us here to flounder on our own, with no human guidance that we can truly trust?

Should we believe the pastor who, meaning to be humble, says he shouldn't be trusted (though he implies his Scriptural understandings can be coming from the Holy Spirit).[134]

Should we believe that our Father would leave us without unity, as Billy Graham puts it, with a "number of local churches formed into various denominations and societies or councils"?

Our Father, in His love and wisdom did not leave us in this quandary. He left us with One Faith and One Church. The Bible tells us so.

We need to trust like we need water! I mean to really trust in a down-to-earth way. Just as our hearts crave so to trust in a family member or friend, all the more so do we need for our hearts to bubble-up-and-out in trust with all that is in us, that which is good, and that which is not good; oh my, oh my, especially is this so in the most important of matters which are the spiritual. We can grasp how beautiful and meaningful trust is, as we look upon the trust, which goes hand-in-hand, with the love

---

[134] ... but in the same breath, saying that God is interpreting the Scriptures to him by his asking of the Holy Spirit.

and peacefulness of mind and heart that a baby has in its mother. So too it is for us that we have human trust in what is to be believed in our Christian faith; just as the parishioners did so confidently in that ole time religion towards the teaching authority of the apostles.

The Baptist Pastor who says to spiritually trust no one somehow fails to see the irrational implications in what he professes and teaches as truth to his parishioners. It seems to me that because he cannot trust in anyone spiritually here on earth, he lives encompassed in a faith that is humanly isolated and alone (I do like this man, and feel that he has a lot of heart, but his doctrines and rationale do not make sense to me).

Some say trusting in human authority in our wanting of truth is the giving-up of one's mind and individuality; but rather we trust in Christ by trusting His commissioning the apostles to establish a church, having a hierarchy, with authority, to guide us in one accord (1Cor.1:10). The preaching I hear of trusting no institution, no religion, is so wrong! Quite the contrary, the ways and means to the truth is trust: For as we see of the scriptural authors, whom we trust, God did convey perfect Truth through imperfect people.

Wanna experience what trust, raw trust, *feels* like? I mean really experience it, really sense it. As a Catholic, go to the sacrament of reconciliation and dare to believe you are really loved, as you repentantly confess those things you would tell no one; opening yourself with a childlike faith, laying out all the dark truth of yourself to the Light, with no righteousness, no denial and evasions, no excuses

... for here in this sacrament there is an invitation for a trust in God's love in all our ways and weaknesses; and to know that anything you speak to this Christ-ordained-presbyter is sealed, by his vow, and with his life. To hear then from him the words of absolution, brings the forgiveness that comes from Christ down to a human-level experience (God knew such means will be best for us in our earthly nature), and to grasp within your heart that "Jesus really does love sinners." [135]

Our conscience compels us to bow our heads down, and we raise them up again by the mercy of Christ. Thus do we, in making a good confession, come to face ourselves in truth, noticing our ways of pride, perhaps our condescension or condemnations of others for one reason or another, or perhaps a self-centeredness and pretentiousness which may taint our hearts; perhaps how we may be motivated by profit, or power, or pleasure. It's here in the confessional that you put on the line your belief in a loving God, in His love, a love you believe is unconditional and, by faith, have a belief in the ordination of spiritual powers to the apostles by Christ.

"Peace be unto you: as my *Father hath sent me, even so send I you."* spoke Christ to His apostles. [136] Thus here did Christ bestow upon them what His Father had

---

[135] Of course, not the sin. Again to say, one's confession is so absolutely sealed, that upon leaving this sacrament, the priest is not at liberty to make mention of it even to the penitent. Oh yes, you may say in jest, that "what happens in Vegas stays in Vegas"; but certainly not in jest, what is spoken in the confessional - stays in the confessional.

[136] Jn.20:21, 17:18.

bestowed upon Him: His ministry of love, healing, reconciliation, and the message and knowledge of truth.

Speaking for myself, the more I've come to trust and allow my heart to open in the confessional (and let there be no doubt, for me it is with timidity), the more inner peace I've come to have, the greater my hope is for eternal salvation, and a much deepened sense of faith in God's love; in the Scriptures; and in Christ. Thanks be to God for this powerful and liberating means of peace and trust. How great a real peace of heart, mind, and soul there is in being Catholic!

* * *

After all is said and done, as said before, it comes down to "Who do you trust?" You may trust your pastor, and thus bring to him, for instance, your question on salvation as mentioned in this book as not being fixed. In recognizing that this is a serious matter, you do so sincerely to seek the truth about it.

What might he say to you?

First off he may likely quote the Biblical verses, Jn.5:13, Jn.6:47, and Rom.816 which he believes in his heart do express God's promise of salvation. They read: *"These things have I written unto you that believe on the name of the Son God: that ye may know that ye have eternal life, and that ye may believe on the name of the Son of God." ... "Verily, verily, I say unto you, he that believeth on me hath everlasting life." ... "The Spirit himself beareth witness with our spirit, that we are the children of God."* Thus will he say to you that this is Biblical proof of a fixed salvation.

He may as well present to you further reasoning that this is Biblical truth (taken from a blog):[137]

> When you receive Jesus Christ as your Lord and Saviour, you enter into a relationship with God. You become a child of God (Jn.1:12). You are born into a family (Jn.3:3–7). The Bible compares this spiritual birth into God's family with the physical birth into your earthly family. When you were born as the child of your father and mother, a relationship was established. Even though you may disown your parents, or they disown you, you cannot change the relationship—they are still your parents and you are still their child...

> Some would argue and say our relationship with God is broken when we sin and we cease to be His child. This is simply not true. Our fellowship with God is broken, but not our relationship. When David had committed adultery and murder, he prayed in confession to God, *"Restore unto me the joy of thy salvation"* (Psalm 51:12). He did not pray, "Restore unto me thy salvation." He did not need to, David's relationship with God had not been altered, just his fellowship and joy.

He goes on to say, "God does not want you to live in a fog. He wants you to know that you are His child."

---

[137] Ministry127.com

The reasoning presented by this pastor is not irrational.[138] But is it true? Let's presume this is your Protestant or Baptist pastor: How do you know if what he says here to you is true to God's word? Might you ask by what authority does he proclaim that his understandings of the Scriptures are correct, and thus that he speaks the Truth? Perhaps you seek an answer to this by knowing of the history of the denomination which he is in; or in knowing of his extensive study of theology; maybe it's in knowing of his deep prayerfulness, or knowing of his exemplary way of life, that leads you to believe what he says.

Along comes another pastor, at another church ... he speaks differently on the matter of salvation. He too quotes the Bible, and he too presents a reasoning that is rational. Why not trust what he has to say? There are many that do. He too may have extensive study in theology; maybe he has a doctoral degree in Biblical studies, and speaks forcefully in a convincing manner; or maybe he simply gives a good sermon with much elaboration; he too may be very prayerful, and leads an exemplary life. Those that attend his church think yours is in error; and those attending yours think they are in error.

So how do you choose one over the other as presenting the Truth? And as you do make your choice, why do you make that choice? Do you make your choice by looking upon any of the pastor's attributes mentioned?

---

[138] Fair to say, I trust, neither is the reasoning presented in this book.

Or do you look upon your own Biblical knowledge? Your own prayerfulness, or your own moral goodness? Or might you rather choose the one that agrees with your own views on the matter of salvation?

"God does not want you to live in a fog. He wants you to know that you are His child." says this pastor in his blog. Yet here you are, God's child, having to make this choice of whose truth to believe?

And so it is, because each and every pastor, and each and every denomination, makes claim to their own Scriptural interpretations as "the Truth", indeed you are left in a fog, and left there to grope about on your own ... for where there is for you no completely trusted single human authority of the Truth, there is no hope of ever being out of the fog.

Thus do I end this book by saying that the personal freedom which we should long for, and strive for, is to be joined together in one accord as commanded by Paul. Our separations and discord impair our faith and are an affliction upon all of Christianity, and a detriment to the mission of Christ.

Thus do I hope that you may have the faith to trust that which God has placed in human hands for our spiritual guidance ... just as did the learned man in Acts8:31: For when he was asked by the apostle if he understood the Scriptures he was reading, he replied:

"How can I, except some man should guide me?"

Amen

That We

Be

one

Jesus prays that we may be one—sharing His glory and love—as He and the Father are one—sharing glory and love.

* Epilogue *

With the greatest of hope, I do pray that you who read this book, by the heartfelt persuasions of the Holy Spirit, will come to embracing the truth of the faith catholic. It is really beyond me to have such hope merely from what I write here, for, as amply said, I am so deficient, and am in no way a theologian, nor a historian, nor am I holy; still I pray so, for there ought be no other reason for me to write this book than to want for the unity of the Christian faithful.

The importance, and truly the consequence of this unity, is not "for the Catholic Church per se", it is for inspiration and reinforcement to mankind that salvation is in Christ; for as He prayed that we be one in Jn.17:21, Jesus went on to speak of its consequence, *"... that the world may believe that thou hast sent me."*

As for my daring hope of this book's illumination of the truth of His Church, there is a personal belief of mine, in an innermost, unexplainable, even indefensible of a way, of someone in particular who I believe will become Catholic as she comes to examine the tenets of the faith on her own, instead of relying on those outside of the Catholic Church for her understanding. Should this be, she will be a moving force by her deep faith in Christ and bring about an advancement in unity among the faithful (this teenage girl, I do ponder, could become a saint of God's Church, for her faith, as I have witnessed, is so genuine and deep). All glory to God.

I love God (albeit, all imperfectly, and sorry to admit, not always with utmost consistency). I love truth, and sought it as I did so sincerely many years ago as I cried out, in anguish and determination, "I want to know the truth!!!" And I now want to open my heart to you that you can be mindful of such Catholic explanations that have been presented here, and it's challenges to the Baptist and Protestant faiths ... not to destroy them, but to bring them to a deeper fullness of faith in Jesus Christ that is in His Church.

Create a clean heart in me, oh God.

That We

Be

one

(Established by the Church's Nicene Council in the year 325 A.D.)

* The Nicene Creed of the Catholic/Universal Faith *

I believe in one God
the Father almighty
maker of heaven and earth
of all things visible and invisible.

I believe in one Lord, Jesus Christ
the only begotten Son of God
born of the Father before all ages.

God from God, Light from Light
true God from true God
begotten, not made, consubstantial with the Father
through him all things were made.

For us men and for our salvation, He came down from heaven
and by the Holy Spirit was incarnate of the virgin Mary
and became man.

For our sake He was crucified under Pontius Pilate
He suffered death and was buried
and rose again on the third day
in accordance with the Scriptures.

He ascended into heaven
and is seated at the right hand of the father
He will come again in glory
To judge the living and the dead
And His kingdom will have no end.

I believe in the Holy Spirit, the Lord, the giver of life
Who proceeds from the Father and the Son
Who with the Father and the Son is adored and glorified
Who has spoken through the prophets.

I believe in one holy catholic and apostolic church
I confess one baptism for the forgiveness of sins
and I look forward to the resurrection of the dead
and the life of the world to come.

Amen.

149

That We

Be

one

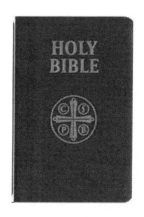

* Suggested Readings *

The 'Douay-Rheims Bible'
Newsletters of 'The Coming Home Network' (chnetwork.org)
'Catholic for A Reason' ... Dr. Scott Hahn & Leon Suprenant Jr.
'Rome Sweet Home' ... Scott & Kimberly Hahn
'Surprised By Truth 1 & 2' ... Patrick Madrid
'Why Be Catholic' ... Richard Rohr & Joseph Martos
'Where We Got the Bible' ... Henry G. Graham

* References *

'The King James Bible'
Pub: Broadman & Holdman 1996

'If Protestantism Is True'... Devin Rose
Pub: Unitas Books 2011

'The Light of Faith'... Pope Francis
Pub: Ignatius Press 2013

'Peace With God'... Billy Graham
Pub: World Publishing 1953

'Where Is That In the Bible'... Patrick Madrid
Pub: Our Sunday Visitor 2001

'Love Unveiled' ... Dr. Edward Sri
Pub: Ignatius Press 2015

'Making Sense of Mary'... Gary G. Michuta
Pub: Grotto Press 2013

'If I'm Christian Why Be Catholic?'... James E. Hanson
Pub: Paulist Press 1984

'Evangelical Is Not Enough'... Thomas Howard
Pub: Ignatius Press 1984

'The Splendor of Truth'... Pope John Paul II
Pub: Pauline Books & Media 1993

'Martin Luther'... Elsie Singmaster & Martin Marty
Pub: Bible Life - pre 1923

'A Testimonial To Grace' ... Avery Dulles, S. J.
Pub: Sheed & Ward 1918

Works of G.K. Chesterton, Vol. 3
(used by permission: Ignatius Press 1926)

'NINE DAYS That Changed the World'
DVD: Hosted by former House Speaker Newt Gingrich& & wife Callista

Wikipedia.com

That We

Be

one

Pray like Jesus

For your interest, here below is the word-cloud of this book:

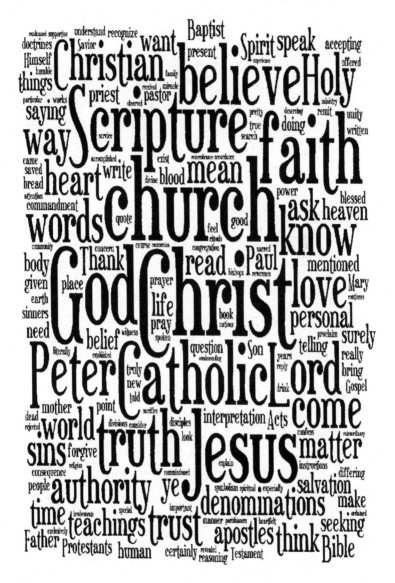

Made in the USA
Charleston, SC
20 May 2016